C I T Y P A C K
Hong Kong

By Sean Sheehan and Pat Levy

3RD EDITION

Fodor's Travel Publications
New York • Toronto • London • Sydney • Auckland

WWW.FODORS.COM

Contents

About this book 4

About this book

KEY TO SYMBOLS

✚ Map reference to the location on the fold-out map accompanying this book

✉ Address

☎ Telephone number

🕐 Opening times

🍴 Restaurant or café on premises or nearby

🚇 Nearest Mass Transit Railway (MTR) subway station

🚃 Nearest overground train station

🚌 Nearest bus/tram route

⛴ Nearest ferry stop

♿ Facilities for visitors with disabilities

✋ Admission charge

↔ Other nearby places of interest

❓ Tours, lectures, or special events

▶ Indicates the page where you will find a fuller description

ℹ Tourist information

Citypack Hong Kong is divided into six sections to cover the six most important aspects of your visit to Hong Kong.

- An overview of the city and its people
- Itineraries, walks, and excursions
- The top 25 sights to visit
- Features about different aspects of the city that make it special
- Detailed listings of restaurants, hotels, stores, and nightlife
- Practical information

In addition, text boxes provide fascinating extra facts and snippets, highlights of places to visit, and practical advice.

CROSS-REFERENCES

To help you make the most of your visit, cross-references, indicated by ▶, show you where to find additional information about a place or subject.

MAPS

The fold-out map in the wallet at the back of the book is a comprehensive street plan of Hong Kong. All the map references given in the book refer to this map. For example, the University Museum at 94 Bonham Road has the following information: ✚ B8 indicating the grid square of the map in which the museum will be found.

The city-center maps found on the inside front and back covers of the book itself are for quick reference. They show the Top 25 Sights, described on pages 24–48, which are clearly plotted by number (**1** – **25**, not page number) from west to east across the city.

ADMISSION CHARGES

An indication of the admission charge for sights is given by categorizing the standard adult rate as follows: ✋ expensive (more than HK$15), ✋ moderate (HK$8–HK$15), and ✋ inexpensive (under HK$8).

HONG KONG *life*

INTRODUCING HONG KONG

Post 1997

On the surface, little has changed since the territory reverted to Chinese rule. "Two systems, one nation" has become a reassuring mantra for those who feared the collapse of Hong Kong's prosperity, and some say Hong Kong is now the model to which the rest of China aspires. However, the people of Hong Kong have enough political savvy to know that the years ahead are still uncertain.

Hong Kong, so long a vestigial colony of the bygone British Empire, reverted to Chinese rule at midnight on June 30, 1997. The pragmatic citizens of Hong Kong took the transition in their stride and life is now back to normal while people wait to see what history will bring. China's entry into the World Trade Organization, due in late 2001, may alter the role of Hong Kong. Although the handover is in the past, the changes are ongoing. In this unfolding drama a visitor to Hong Kong can share.

From an urban aesthetic perspective Hong Kong Island is visually stunning. In the Central area an astonishing array of skyscrapers peer down on a contradictory mix of the materialistic and the spiritual. In the parks people are practicing *t'ai chi ch'uan*, the gently flowing balletic movements that get the life energy moving smoothly around the body. Yet while half the city seems to be practicing this slow-motion martial art, the other half are speed walking—herding in a mad dash to their offices.

Whether it is rush hour or midday, do not expect politeness on the streets or on the trains. People are constantly pushed out of the way and

bounce off one another like human pinballs. Everywhere they are frantically trying to make money. Meanwhile, some things never change; beneath an underpass you may find an old woman crouching to beat, with a shoe, a piece of paper that carries the names of her gossipy neighbors, whose malicious influence will, she hopes, be crushed by this ancient magic ritual of *da siu yan* (beating small people).

Sharing the incredibly congested space with financial institutions and shopping centers are public housing projects, eyesores that are home to ordinary citizens whose lives have little in common with the glitz and glamor all over the city. In Hong Kong the best and the worst are shambled on top of each other. Many of the older housing deveolpments—even on Hong Kong island, which is home to the wealthiest tycoons—look unfinished outside; inside, on the other hand some apartments are right out of a *chi chi* home decor magazine. On Victoria Peak, the wooded 1,800-foot-high hill that looks down on Central and Victoria Harbour from the center of the island, you will find the homes of the rich and famous—paying some of the city's highest rents. But from the summit, the view takes in

Live to work

The work ethic is not an ideal in Hong Kong, it is simply a necessity of life. There are virtually no natural resources, only some 386 square miles of land, and no unemployment pay or minimum wages.

The Star Ferry crosses the harbor, linking Kowloon and Hong Kong Island

Gweilos

The literal translation for *gweilo* is "ghost man" (*gweipor* means "ghost woman"), originally coined as a derogatory label for the pale-faced colonial masters. You can tell by the tone of voice if it is still meant in a derogatory manner, but usually nowadays it is used as a general references for Westerners whose presence in areas such as Wan Chai, especially at night, seems disproportionate given that they constitute less than 2 percent of the population.

dilapidated buildings that seem to be a stone's throw away. Here, owning a Rolls Royce is a status symbol. But so is needing a lawn mower.

Hong Kong Island is only one part of Hong Kong. Five minutes by ferry across the harbor lies the tip of the Kowloon Peninsula, called Tsim Sha Tsui—TST for short. Here ritzy and not-so-ritzy stores and restaurants are packed together with a staggering density. Business is cutthroat, and persistent touts harass you forcing brochures on you about where to get a suit custom-made or buy a pashmina shawl that just went on sale last week.

North of Tsim Sha Tui is the residential and shopping area Mong Kok, which has the highest population density on earth. By day it is a shopping haven; at night its brothels draw local Hong Kongers. No matter what time you visit, you will literally rub shoulders with the residents and share the frustrations and frissons of a truly frenetic lifestyle. While visitors often find it exhausting, locals are nonplussed; they are used to living and working in cramped quarters, and have developed strategies for being alone in crowded places. Caught up in their own private mobile telephone conversations or daydreams they often don't even realize they've collided with you.

Still, there are places where you can escape from the hustle and bustle. North in the New Territories, which stretch up to the border with China, life has a slower pace. In some of the islands and in coastal towns like Sai Kung, you find western enclaves of expats who have escaped to this seaside with a mountainous backdrop where life is much more like mainland China than central Hong Kong. Today post 1997, most Hong Kong people are tied to their forebears across the border more closely than ever, and it is this cultural continuity that gives Hong Kong its unique appeal and fascination. This is no mere Chinatown; it is a Chinese city with pockets of Westernism where you can enjoy the best of both worlds.

HONG KONG IN FIGURES

Culture and Recreation

- Hong Kong's 7 million people squeeze into just 386 square miles.
- 80 percent of Hong Kong's territory is rural or country park.
- 40 percent of the land is conserved in country parks (the highest ratio in the world).
- The world's largest indoor Chinese restaurant is the Ocean City Restaurant, which can cater for more than 6,000 guests.
- The world's largest floating restaurants (the Jumbo and the Sea Palace) are in Aberdeen Harbour on the south side of Hong Kong Island.
- Seven of the world's ten busiest McDonald's restaurants are in Hong Kong.

Economics and Society

- Under the Sino-British Joint Declaration, Hong Kong retains its existing social and economic system for at least 50 years.
- Hong Kong is the world's leading exporter of watches, clothing, and imitation jewelry.
- Hong Kong is Asia's leading gold distribution center and third largest gold bullion market.

World Records

- More than half of the city's 7 million inhabitants live in public housing.
- Over 9 million books are borrowed from Hong Kong's public libraries every year (one of the world's highest per capita readerships).
- Despite being the third most densely populated place on earth, only Sweden and Japan have lower infant and child death rates.
- At 121 yards by 21 yards, the advertising sign for Nanfang Pharmaceutical Factory's "999" traditional Chinese medicine is the world's largest neon sign. With over 8 miles of neon tubing, it took half a year to construct.

Leading Consumers

- Hong Kong is per capita the world's leading consumer of oranges.
- Hong Kong is per capita the world's leading consumer of cognac.
- Hong Kong has the highest per capita ownership of Rolls Royce cars in the world.
- Hong Kong has the highest ratio of cafés and restaurants to population in the world.

A CHRONOLOGY

4000 BC | Early settlements left some pottery, stone tools, and iron implements—then for many centuries the islands had more pirates than farmers.

AD 25 | An approximate date for the Han Dynasty Lei Cheng Uk Tomb in Kowloon (► 35). The Chinese Empire had been unified a couple of hundred years earlier, and for the next millennium and a half the area around Hong Kong Island was ruled by a governor based in Canton (Guangzhou) to the north.

1685 | Canton was opened to European trade, and British and French merchants began to deal in tea and silk. The British later started to import opium as a way of extending their power and profits. Two early traders were William Jardine and James Matheson, both from Scotland.

1841 | Chinese attempts to block the import of opium ended in their defeat; the treaty concluding the first Opium War ceded Hong Kong Island to the British "in perpetuity." Within two decades, another treaty conceded the Kowloon Peninsula, again "in perpetuity."

1898 | A further treaty, in 1898, leased substantial land north of Kowloon—the New Territories—to Britain for 99 years.

1937–45 | Throughout 1937, hundreds of thousands of Chinese, displaced by the Japanese invasion of China, sought refuge in Hong Kong. On December 8, 1941, Japanese aircraft bombed Kowloon, and by Christmas Day the British had surrendered. Over 2,000 people died and 10,000 soldiers were taken prisoner. British civilians were incarcerated in Stanley Prison. With the surrender of the Japanese in August, 1945, Hong Kong again became a British colony.

1947–67 | The years around the 1949 Communist victory in China saw further refugee influxes. The population doubled within 14 years, and when the United States imposed sanctions against China during the Korean War (1950–53), the colony developed a manufacturing base of its own. China periodically called for the return of its land. In 1962, over 70,000 Chinese crossed the border.

1967 The political passions rocking China during its Cultural Revolution spilled over into Hong Kong in the form of riots and strikes, and the colony seemed on the brink of a premature closure of its lease, but normality soon returned.

1975 100,000 refugees arrived from Vietnam.

1982 British Prime Minister Margaret Thatcher went to Beijing to discuss the colony's future with Deng Xiaoping. China made no secret of its wish to be reunited with all of Hong Kong.

1984–88 The Sino-British Joint Declaration in 1984 confirmed the return of the colony to China. In 1988 Beijing published its Basic Law for Hong Kong citizens, guaranteeing their rights.

1989 The Tiananmen Square massacre in June served only to confirm Hong Kong's worst fears about the future under China's sovereignty. Over a million people took to the streets in an unprecedented protest against Beijing, and the stock market fell by over 20 percent in one day.

1997 "The Handover." On July 1, Hong Kong became a Special Administrative Region of China. English remains an official language. People from other parts of China require special approval for entry.

1998 Turmoil in Asian stock markets delivered a blow to Hong Kong. Many expatriates working in the money markets were sent home. In July a new international airport opened at a cost of billions of dollars after almost ten years of land reclamation and reconstruction.

2000–2001 Hong Kong businessmen prepare for mainland China's potential entry into the World Trade Organization (WTO).

PEOPLE & EVENTS FROM HISTORY

Chris Patten, last British governor of Hong Kong

The 14K and the Bamboo Union

The names of the Triad Secret Societies may sound intriguing, but the reality of life in these secret societies is sordid. Promised easy money and social acceptance, disaffected youths of both sexes are lured into these groups, which control organized crime in Hong Kong. Unless they leave very soon, they are drawn into an organization with a lifetime membership. While triads are thriving in Hong Kong, it is unlikely tourists or even expats will encounter them. After all, not every teenager with blond hair and a tattoo is a member.

CHRIS PATTEN

Hong Kong's last British governor was its most controversial. At first his appointment in 1993 seemed auspicious: his name in Chinese implied good luck. However, he soon caused consternation by establishing a democratic Hong Kong Assembly—controversial because it drew attention to previous British administrations that had never felt any need to govern Hong Kong democratically. Casting caution to the wind, Patten gave Hong Kong citizens, for the first time, the right to elect Assembly representatives. The Chinese threatened to renege on outstanding contracts after the handover. But things settled down, and when the day came Patten and family acquitted themselves well.

THE HANDOVER

At midnight on June 30, 1997, Britain's last vestige of empire was handed back to the Chinese. Trepidation surrounded the occasion, but in the event, it was a muted affair in one of the worst rainstorms in memory. Few people were on the streets, the Patten family and Prince Charles quietly slipped away on the royal yacht *Britannia* (her last official job) and the Red Army silently drove across the border to take up their new homes. The expatriate workers who had not chosen to leave celebrated in Lan Kwai Fong bars, and everyone woke up the next day a little nervously, wondering how their lives would be changed, and a little shocked that nothing seemed different.

TUNG CHEE-HWA

Chief Executive Tung Chee-hwa, who took office in 1997, was a shipping magnate before taking office. He weathered some shaky years in business; the inherited Tung empire suffered a major setback in the early 1980s as the global economic recession knocked the shipping industry. Some reports say company debts reached HK$20 billion and critics speculate that money pumped into the company came from the mainland. Thus, Mr. Tung became indebted to Beijing and is the perfect puppet leader as a result.

HONG KONG
how to organize your time

ITINERARIES

You can see the essential sights of Hong Kong in just four days. The city, on Hong Kong Island, is compact and can be covered in a day; Kowloon's museums and shops deserve a day's attention; you can tour the southern side of Hong Kong Island another day; and try to visit an outlying island.

ITINERARY ONE	**HONG KONG ISLAND: THE CITY**
Morning	Make an early morning trip to the Peak (► 27), then visit Sheung Wan (► 17), with its snake restaurants and medicine shops.
Afternoon	The tranquil Botanical Gardens (► 32) and the intriguing Hong Kong Park (► 37) make for a quiet break.
Evening	See Lan Kwai Fong, the trendy nightlife area, with a cluster of bars and restaurants.
ITINERARY TWO	**HONG KONG ISLAND: THE SOUTH SHORE**
Morning	You can get to Stanley (► 48) via a spectacular double-decker bus ride. Spend a morning at the beach or browsing around the market.
Lunch	At one of the floating restaurants in Aberdeen Harbour (► 33).
Afternoon	Explore Aberdeen.
Evening	Stroll around Wan Chai (if you are not traveling with kids) or Soho; there are plenty of bars (► 83) and restaurants (► 62–69) in both areas.
ITINERARY THREE	**LANTAU ISLAND**
Morning	Go when the weather is good since all your time is spent outdoors. The idyllic, hour-long boat trip past a sea of moored ships, tiny islands, and colorful catamarans ends at Lantau Island. Visit Po Lin Monastery, where a huge Buddha statue (► 24) dominates the landscape, see the spectacular temples and tea gardens, and walk along the Lantau Trail.
Lunch	In Tai O, the tiny fishing village on stilts.

Afternoon	Sightseeing in Tai O.
Evening	Discovery Bay, with rocking nightlife, followed by a starlit journey back to the city.
ITINERARY FOUR	KOWLOON
Morning	Since much of what you see is undercover, you can do this tour even when it's rainy. Museums close only on major public holidays. Start in Kowloon Park to see *t'ai chi ch'uan* exercises and to visit the Hong Kong Museum of History (➤ 39). The Museum of Art (➤ 43) and Space Museum (➤ 42) are both nearby in the Hong Kong Cultural Centre on the waterfront.
Afternoon	Prowl around Kowloon's shops. Catch the jade market at Temple Street before it closes at 3PM (➤ 41), and squeeze in a trip to the Lei Cheng Uk Museum (➤ 35) or Wong Tai Sin Temple (➤ 46).
Evening	Take a trip down one of the night markets (➤ 41) and then dine *al fresco* on seafood at a market restaurant.

Buddha statue, Po Lin Monastery, Lantau Island

15

WALKS

THE SIGHTS

- Bowen Road shrines
- Mid Levels
- Lover's Stone Garden
- Police Museum (➤ 59)
- Covered market
- Meat and fish stands along Wan Chai Road

INFORMATION

Distance 2 miles
Time 2 hours
Start point Bowen Road
➕ G10
🚌 15 from Central Bus Terminal or Peak Terminal; get off at the Adventist Hospital at the horseshoe bend where Bowen Road meets Stubbs Road
End point Johnston Road
➕ F8
🚋 Wan Chai
🚌 Tram stop on Johnston Road

ALONG THE QUIET MID LEVELS OF THE PEAK, THEN INTO HECTIC WAN CHAI

Shady and quiet, Bowen Road runs along the Mid Levels on Hong Kong Island, a residential area halfway up Victoria Peak; note the small roadside shrines. Walk west for 15 minutes, then look for steps on the left up to an exposed rock shrine (Lover's Stone Garden) via a small complex of incense-burning pots. Continue along Bowen Road as far as Wan Chai Gap Road. Detour left, to Stubbs Road and the Police Museum. Or continue right, along the main walk, down steep Wan Chai Gap Road. At the bottom, turn right onto Kennedy Road and then left onto Queen's Road East. Turn right at the covered market onto bustling Wan Chai Road.

Turn left onto Johnston Road; pause for traditional herbal tea at No. 137, next to the Simsons Commercial Building. For lunch, try Indian cuisine at the International Curry House on Tai Wong Street East, or at the Jo Jo Mess Club (➤ 66), entered on Lee Tung Street, both left turns off Johnston Road.

One block to the south is Hennessy Road, where there are plenty of fast-food eateries.

Fish stand in Wan Chai Road

THE HEART OF HONG KONG

Start this walk at Western Market, once the local "wet," or fresh food, market, opposite Macau Ferry Pier on Hong Kong Island; built in 1906 and renovated in 1991, it is now an arts and crafts center. Head south, uphill, then turn right onto Wing Lok Street, a traditional trading street with neon signs, aging buildings, and a variety of flourishing trades. Turning back along Bonham Strand West, notice the flashy new ginseng wholesalers that still have huge traditional lanterns and painted signboards.

Inspect the food on sale in Sheung Wan Market; for an adventure, visit the top floor and sample some local dishes. Along Bonham Strand East and Queen's Road West there are many antiques stores and shops selling calligraphy materials, wedding clothes, and funeral paraphernalia. Queen's Road has the big stores.

At Peel Street, turn uphill and wander through the street market, which sells all manner of foreign things. Turn right onto Hollywood Road, part of Sheung Wan, and admire the applied arts shops. The Man Mo Temple is on this road; turn right down Ladder Street, which leads to Upper Lascar Row and more antiques, curios, and junk merchants. From here, go downhill to return to the walk's starting point, taking in on the way Possession Street, where the British flag was first raised.

THE SIGHTS

- Western Market
- Bonham Strand West ginseng traders (► 29)
- Sheung Wan Market
- Bonham Strand East antique shops (► 29)
- Man Mo Temple (► 30)
- Possession Street

INFORMATION

Distance 2 miles
Time 2 hours
Start and end point Western Market
- D7
- Sheung Wan
- Any tram from Central

Antiques shop

EVENING STROLLS

INFORMATION

Distance ¾ mile
Time 30 minutes
Start point Wan Chai Star Ferry
🚇 F8
🚊 Wan Chai
End point Wan Chai MTR
🚇 F8
🚊 Wan Chai
🚌 Trams to Causeway Bay and
Sheung Wan

INFORMATION

Distance 1 mile
Time 30 minutes
Start point Star Ferry Terminal,
Tsim Sha Tsui, Kowloon
🚇 F7
End point Kowloon Railway
Terminal
🚇 G6
🚌 Buses and taxis are plentiful

*Clock tower outside Star
Ferry terminal*

THE ELEVATED WALKWAY OF WAN CHAI

From the Wan Chai Star Ferry terminal, Hong Kong Island, take the walkway to find the red China Resources Building (CRB). Below it, and worth a visit, is a Chinese garden. East of the CRB is the Museum of Chinese Historical Relics, made to look like an ancient Chinese building and containing some interesting displays. Retracing your steps takes you past an excellent Chinese products emporium and through the Hong Kong Convention and Exhibition Centre, where you can admire some harbor views. The overhead walk continues through the splendid Central Plaza and the Immigration Tower, and across some of the seedier streets of old Wan Chai. End your stroll at the Wan Chai MTR station.

WATERFRONT PROMENADE OF TSIM SHA TSUI

Outside Star Ferry terminal in Tsim Sha Tsui, Kowloon, is the Clock Tower, all that is left of the Old Kowloon Railway Station, built in 1916 and demolished in 1978. Pass two highly controversial structures: the windowless Hong Kong Cultural Centre, and, across the road, the central extension of the Peninsula Hotel. Most other hotels along this stretch of road are equally unattractive, so

walk to the back of the Hong Kong Space Museum and the Hong Kong Museum of Art. Stroll along the Waterfront Promenade and enjoy glittering night views of Wan Chai and Causeway Bay across the harbor. Rejoin Salisbury Road and continue east as far as the underpass, where you can either turn back or continue to the railroad terminus at Hung Hom.

ORGANIZED SIGHTSEEING

HKTB

The **Hong Kong Tourist Board** (➤ 90) conducts half- and whole-day tours to a number of interesting destinations, as well as themed tours. The HKTB has developed the Quality Tourism Services (QTS) scheme as a pledge of service excellence. Look for those establishments displaying the QTS logo.

SPLENDID TOURS & TRAVEL

Splendid will organize personalized tours of Hong Kong and South China. They will take you shopping, hiking, and even on a helicopter ride over the city. A typical tour, the Hong Kong Island Orientation, takes you to Victoria Peak, Aberdeen Fishing Village, Repulse Bay Lookout, and Stanley Market in one five-hour tour. It costs HK$280 for adults and HK$190 for children. ☎ 2316 2152

WATER TOURS LTD

Conducts nearly 20 different harbor cruises, including a sampan ride around Aberdeen. ☎ 2730 6170

STAR FERRY

Seven ferries a day. ☎ 2366 7024/2324

GRAYLINE TOURS

City tours, dinner cruises, and day trips to China. ☎ 2368 7111

Heritage tour highlight

The Man Mo Temple in Tai Po (➤ 30), part of the HKTB's Heritage Tour, is an especially rich experience on Saturday, when the surrounding street market is abuzz. The ancient gray stone temple, dedicated to the gods of war and literature, offers a calm respite from the market outside. In the market, look for the snakes in the snake soup shops, the partially dissected live fish in the fish stands, and old ladies carrying their wares suspended from a pole across their shoulders.

Sampan ride around Aberdeen Harbour

EXCURSIONS

INFORMATION

Lamma Island
Distance 6 miles
Journey time 50 minutes
📷 Ferry from Central Pier, Central ✚ D7

Hakka women cutting watercress, New Territories

New Territories
Distance Tai Po 16 miles; Sheung Shui 22 miles
Journey time 1 hour
🚇 MTR from any station to Kowloon Tong (✚ F2), where the interchange accesses equally regular KCR trains traveling north to Lo Wu. The last stop is Sheung Shui, less than an hour from Central, which is as far as you can go without traveling on into China.

Hong Kong Railway Museum
🕐 Wed–Mon 9–4

LAMMA ISLAND

This island, whose resident expatriate community has give it a chic, radical, and bohemian image, offers refuge from the concrete jungle as well as a glimpse of a fast-disappearing rural lifestyle. You can have surprisingly good meals at the two ferry villages—Yung Shue Wan and Sok Kwu Wan—and the hour-long walk between them takes in a decent beach, the best of which is Lo So Shing, and scenic viewpoints. In Yung Shue Wan there are a number of craft shops worth a browse.

NEW TERRITORIES

The New Territories are best explored via the Kowloon–Canton Railway (KCR ➤ 90). From Kowloon station the line heads northward, passing a number of interesting stopping points. From either Tai Po Market station or Tai Wo station, take a taxi to the Hong Kong Railway Museum and visit the Man Mo Temple, Tai Po in the adjacent pedestrianized market street. At the next station, Fanling, take the right exit; the Taoist Ying Sin Kwun Temple just across the road is worth a visit, as is the old village just minutes from the next station, Sheung Shui. Take the overhead footway to the right and head down to the bus station. With McDonald's on your right, walk along the main road until you see the old lanes on the left. Life here, only a couple of miles south of the border, is little different from that in the rest of China.

MACAU

Cobbled streets, baroque architecture, and the traditional cuisine and wines of Portugal's last colony are good reasons for taking the trip to Macau, which reverted to China in December, 1999. Macau is compact and most of the main places of interest you can take in in a day. Highlights include the ruined façade of 17th-century St. Paul's Church, the Jesuit Monte Fortress, and a number of old churches and temples. Hotels and good restaurants are easy to find, and prices are agreeably lower than those in Hong Kong.

THE PEOPLE'S REPUBLIC OF CHINA

The Beijing government has designated Shenzen as a Special Economic Zone—and tourists and investors—anyone with money to spend—are welcomed with open arms. Here you'll find Splendid China, a theme park where the Great Wall, the Forbidden City, and other monuments of Chinese architecture are reduced to one-fifthteenth real size. The nearby China Folk Culture village introduces the country's ethnic minorities. Guangzhou (Canton), a major city and port on the Pearl River has been trading with Europeans for 400 years. It offers an astonishing food market, a fascinating 100 BC royal tomb, several temples, and bustling street life.

INFORMATION

Macau
Distance 37 miles
Journey time 1 hour by jetfoil

🚤 Jetfoil from the Shun Tak Centre

➕ D7

✉ 200 Connaught Road, a ten-minute walk west of Central

💰 Jetfoil: HKS130–161

ℹ Tourist office in Macau:
✉ Largo do Senado, Edificio Ritz No 9
☎ (853) 315 566
Tourist office in Hong Kong:
✉ Shop 336, Shun Tak Centre, 200 Connaught Road, Central
☎ 2857 2287

❓ Take your passport; no visa required for North Americans or Europeans who stay 20 days or less

The People's Republic of China
Shenzen can be seen in a day, while Guangzhou (Canton) is best enjoyed with an overnight stay

Shenzen
Distance 25 miles
Journey time 40 minutes

🚆 KCR from Kowloon Tong station to border at Lo Wo

❓ Organized tours: Grayline Tours ☎ 2368 7111

Guangzhou (Canton)
Distance 75 miles
Journey time Under 3 hours by train

🚆 Express train from Hong Kong

❓ Organized tours: Grayline Tours ☎ 2368 7111

St. Paul's, Macau

WHAT'S ON

For details, look for the free *HK Magazine* and the *BC Magazine*. The English newspapers also carry details of events (➤ 91). Chinese Lunar festivals are movable; check dates ahead with the HKTB office (➤ 90).

January/Febraury	*Chinese (Lunar) New Year:* Essentially a family event, this looms large in Hong Kong life. The week before the New Year is intensely busy; the harbor fireworks display is magnificent, but the crowds are enormous.
mid-January/ mid-March	*Arts Festival:* International orchestral, dance, and theater events over three to four weeks at various venues throughout the territory.
late March/April	*International Film Festival:* For two weeks; various venues.
April	*Ching Ming:* Tomb-sweeping day.
	Tin Hau Festival: Tin Hau temples (➤ 53) remember a 12th-century legend, about a girl who saves her brothers from drowning. Fishing junks and temples are decorated and Chinese street operas held near the temples.
	Birthday of Lord Buddha (late Apr): At temples throughout the territory, Buddha's statue is ceremonially bathed and scented (➤ 45), symbolically washing away sins and material encumbrances.
June	*Dragon Boat Festival* : Noisy, colorful dragon-boat races are held to commemorate the political protests of a 4th-century poet and patriot Chu Yuan.
August/September	*Hungry Ghosts Festival:* For a month offerings of food are set out to placate roaming spirits (➤ 35).
September/October	*Mid-Fall Festival* : Families head out with lanterns and eat mooncakes to commemorate a 14th-century uprising against the Mongols.
October/November	*Festival of Asian Arts:* Asian music, dance, and theater in even-numbered years.

HONG KONG's
top 25 sights

The sights are shown on the maps on the inside front cover and inside back cover, numbered **1–25** *from west to east across the city*

PO LIN BUDDHA

HIGHLIGHTS

- Po Lin Buddha
- Tranquil monastery
- Views of the South China Sea and other islands
- A peaceful ferry ride
- Hikes in pristine jungles
- Chance to see the splendor of the island before it is further developed

INFORMATION

➕ Off map to west

✉ Lantau Island

🕐 Temple: Daily 8–8

🚌 Tung Chung and then buses heading for Po Lin

🚢 Ferry from Queen's Pier Central (journey time approx 45 minutes)

🎫 Free (HKTB tour HK$320 per person)

❓ HKTB guided nature walks: Lantau Island—Trails and Temples

Asia's largest outdoor Buddha, the 112-foot tall, 250-ton bronze statue sits regally atop a mountain on Lantau Island. You can spy the Buddha in his meditative pose as you descend into Chek Lap Kok airport.

Worth the trek Even after the airport was built, Lantau remained one of the largest green areas in Hong Kong. It is home to rare species such as the Hong Kong newt and the ayu, a stream-dwelling fish. The island's rocky coastline and jungle mountain scenery make it a bit of an outback. But this isolated outpost is home to almost 300 Buddhist monasteries, most of them tiny temples tucked away in remote areas. The famous Po Lin Buddha is at Po Lin (Precious Lotus) Monastery, halfway up the mountainside on the Ngong Ping Plateau. Established by three monks in 1905 the monastery is now extensively restored. But the real attraction is the huge Buddha, which was completed in 1993 on the hilltop above the monastery. To get up close, you need to climb 268 steps. Up top, you get a splendid view of Lantau and the other little islands dotting the blue-jade South China Sea. There are also trails jutting away from the monastery if you want to go for a longer walk.

Go now On Buddhist holidays up to 13,000 visitors a day make the trek to the Buddha. But at other times, the island feels quite remote, despite the airport (constructed in 1998), which brought a train connection to Kowloon and Hong Kong Island; before then, you could reach the island only by ferry. Now, with plans afoot for developing housing on the island and the opening of a Disney theme park proposed for 2005, there are fears for the ecology and the remoteness of the area.

SAM TUNG UK MUSEUM

The clean, simple lines of this ancient Hakka dwelling stand out against the surrounding forest of high-rise housing projects. Though simple farming people, the Hakka would have had far more space than their ancestors today.

History Around a million people now live in Tsuen Wan, which was a sleepy little waterside village of a few thousand souls until as recently as 1977. Back in the 17th century the area was subject to constant pirate attacks so the inhabitants built walled villages as a defense. Within each village lived the members of a single clan; a Hakka clan called the Chans made their home in Sam Tung Uk. The Hakka, originally from the north of China, moved to southern China in the 12th and 13th centuries, when the Chinese empire stretched to this area because the Chinese emperor was being driven south by invading Mongols. In 1277, the emperor and his entourage arrived in Tsuen Wan. Feuds over land tenure led some Hakka clans to migrate further, to Hong Kong, Taiwan, and Singapore. The village was probably built in 1786.

Three-beam dwelling This translation of the village's name refers to its structure. Three connected halls form the core of village life, and the three rows of houses were supported by three central beams called *tung*. The main ancestral hall is at the front and its design is highly ornate; its original decorations have been restored to their original bright reds and greens. The other two halls, used for daily living, are more rustic. These halls now display farming equipment, period furniture, and kitchen utensils. Outside are a fish pond, a threshing floor, and the gatehouse that guarded the village. The MTR journey out here takes at least one hour.

HIGHLIGHTS

- Ancestral hall with ornate, highly colored decorations
- Landscaped gardens
- Orientation room
- Blackwood furniture
- Cooking equipment
- Gatehouse of walled village
- Fish ponds
- Threshing floor

INFORMATION

- Off map to north
- 2 Kwu Uk Lane, Tsuen Wan, New Territories
- 2411 2001
- Mon, Wed–Sun 9–5
- Tsuen Wan
- 51 from Tai Ho Road North takes you to the hoverferry back to Central
- Few
- Free
- HKTB Heritage tour (► 19), plus private tours

3

UNIVERSITY MUSEUM

INFORMATION

- B8
- 94 Bonham Road, Hong Kong Island
- 2241 5513
- Mon–Sat 9:30–6; Sun 1:30–5:30. Closed public holidays and March 16
- Sheung Wan
- 3 from Rumsey Street in Central or 23 from North Point ferry terminal
- None
- Free

This interesting little collection of predominantly Chinese artifacts is well worth the effort to see it. It is on the University of Hong Kong campus at the end of Bonham Road, and usually blessedly empty.

Nestorian bronze crosses The displays in this out-of-the-way museum, in the university's Fung Ping Shan Building, date from the 5th century BC onwards, but the highlight is a set of 467 Nestorian bronze crosses—the largest such collection in the world—which belonged to a Christian sect that originated in Syria and came to China during the Tang Dynasty (AD 618–906). The crosses date back to the Yuan Dynasty (1280–1367) and were probably worn as part of a belt or as a pendant. They are made in various cross shapes, including swastikas and birds, as well as conventional crucifixes.

Ceramics and bronzes Notable among the other bronze items on display are mirrors from the Warring States period (475–221 BC), and Shang and Zhou ritual vessels and weapons. The museum also houses an enormous collection of ceramics dating back as far as neolithic times. The painted neolithic pottery is very fine, and the Han Dynasty horse is full of life. Look for the three-color glaze Tang pottery, the famous kiln wares of Song, and the polychrome and monochrome ceramics from the Ming and Qing Dynasties.

Beyond Hong Kong Artifacts from other Asian countries include some Indian Buddhist sculptures and items from Thailand, Vietnam, and Korea. Scroll paintings, inlaid blackwood furniture, and a huge bronze drum make up the rest of the collection.

VICTORIA PEAK

Visiting the Peak is one of the first things to do when you get to Hong Kong. At 1,811 feet the hilltop views are spectacular and the area offers some peaceful, shady walks.

Head for heights Some people like to make the pilgrimage up the Peak twice—during the day and again at night, when the full majesty of the city below is spelled out in lights. The Peak is a relatively unspoiled oasis in a concrete jungle, home of the rich and famous, and a good place for a quiet walk or even a strenuous jog.

Top stop The Peak Galleria, is a veritable tourist trap. The Odditorium (400 displays of strange-but-true facts and artifacts), simulated rides, a wax museum, and restaurants in the nearby Peak Tower offer further distractions. The trip up in the Peak Tram, constructed 1888, is good fun as long as you don't have to line up for it for hours—avoid weekends and the first day after a misty spell (and don't forget your camera). Feeding dollars into one of the telescopes is also worth the money on a clear day. From the tram stop you can also walk along Mount Austin Road to Victoria Park Gardens and the ruins of the Governor's Lodge, destroyed by the Japanese in World War II.

HIGHLIGHTS

- Views over Hong Kong
- Tram ride to the top
- Old Governor's Lodge, with toposcope in its gardens
- Souvenirs in Peak Galleria
- Outdoor tables in Peak Café
- Green-arrowed walk up Mount Austin Road

INFORMATION

- C9–D9
- Peak Tower, Peak Road
- Peak Tram: runs 7AM–midnight
  Odditorium: 9AM–10PM
- Peak Galleria (snacks) and Peak Café
- Trams run every 10–15 minutes from terminals at Garden Road and Cotton Tree Drive.
  Central Bus 15 from Central Bus Terminal to Victoria Gap.
  Minibus 1 from H.M.S. *Tamar*
- Good
- Tram fare: moderate
  Peak Tower: free
  Odditorium: moderate
- Botanical & Zoological Gardens (▶ 32)
  Hong Kong Park (▶ 37)

Souvenir shopping in the Peak Galleria

27

5

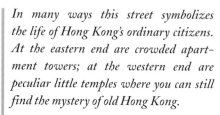

TAI PING SHAN STREET

HIGHLIGHTS

- Views down alleyways leading to Des Voeux Road
- Street temples with gold-painted doorway carvings
- Shops and stands around temples
- Hollywood Garden
- Church in shopping block

INFORMATION

Carving over temple door

In many ways this street symbolizes the life of Hong Kong's ordinary citizens. At the eastern end are crowded apartment towers; at the western end are peculiar little temples where you can still find the mystery of old Hong Kong.

Backstreet buildings South of Hollywood Road and its touristy antiques and curio shops lies Tai Ping Shan Street, a quiet backwater of crumbling 1950s apartments, car-repair workshops, and narrow, stepped alleys that lead north through street markets. At the western end, what seems to be a dead end becomes another narrow, stepped alley with tiny temples on either side.

Temple life Inside the street's temples, the atmosphere may seem, to an outsider, less than pious, with people shaking their fortunes out of bamboo pots to have them read by interpreters, visitors bringing offerings of thanks, and others just lounging about passing the time of day. However, nothing here is in English—these are serious places where a woman may come to ask for children or seek promotion at work. Like most temples in Hong Kong, these ones like to hedge their bets by paying homage to the Buddhist pantheon as well as to Taoist gods. Chinese religion is essentially pragmatic; if the gods turn up the goods then they must be paid. Around the temple are stands selling things the gods appreciate, such as joss sticks, incense candles, paper figures, and fake paper or "hell" money to be burned and sent up in smoke for the dead to spend in the next world.

6

BONHAM STRAND

Bonham Strand is full of cafés and shops that sell dishes such as snake's gall bladder wine and warming, strengthening snake soup—liver-colored, thick, and meaty in texture. The best time to visit is in winter, when the Chinese believe in consuming strong, hearty food.

Bonham Strand East Cafés are concentrated in the eastern section of Bonham Strand. If you wait around, you can watch the victims being chosen and skinned on the pavement before they are put into the cooking pot. The snakes and a few other creatures await their fate in cages on the sidewalk. In some shops, lizards, and turtles sit alongside cobras, pythons, and other deadly creatures. The deadlier the snake, the more powerful its medicinal value is believed to be.

Bonham Strand West To reach the western half of Bonham Strand, you need to walk down Wing Lok Street. This area is great place to wander. Ginseng wholesalers share the road here with some prosperous-looking banks. Most of the quaint old wooden interiors of the former have now given way to glass and chrome, but the jars of unidentifiable items are still there. Ginseng means "man" in Chinese, so-called as the forked root resembles a person. Esteemed for its power as a universal panacea to heal and promote good health, it is an expensive commodity and much wheeler-dealing goes on over its price. Different types of ginseng bring different prices, the American variety being the cheapest while ginseng from Korea and China is considered more efficacious and is therefore more expensive. Turn to the left off Bonham Strand West and you will find Queen's Road West with shops selling bird's nests—for the soup.

HIGHLIGHTS

- Snake shop at No. 127 Bonham Strand East
- Ginseng wholesalers on Bonham Strand West
- Chinese medicine shops in Ko Shing Street
- Street barbers in Sutherland Street
- Nearby Possession Street, marking the place where Hong Kong was claimed by the British
- Nearby Queen's Road West selling bird's nests
- Sheung Wan Market

INFORMATION

- ✚ D7
- ✉ Bonham Strand, Sheung Wan
- 🕐 Stores close on public holidays, particularly Chinese New Year
- 🍴 Food stands in Sheung Wan Market and streets around Bonham Strand; fast food near MTR station
- 🚇 Sheung Wan
- 🚋 Trams stop at Western Market and go on through Central to Causeway Bay
- 🅖 Good
- 💰 Free
- ↔ Tai Ping Shan Street (▶ 28)
  Man Mo Temple (▶ 30)

7

MAN MO TEMPLE

- Statues of Man Cheong and Kuan Ti
- Sedan chairs once used to carry statues
- Embroideries surrounding statues
- Drum and bell on right of entrance door
- Soot-blackened deities on left of entrance door
- Gold and brass standards carried during parades
- Resident fortune-tellers

INFORMATION

- ✚ D8
- ✉ Junction of Hollywood Road and Ladder Street
- 🕐 Daily 7–5
- 🚇 Sheung Wan
- ♿ Access difficult
- 🎫 Free
- ↔ Tai Ping Shan Street (➤ 28)
  Bonham Strand East and West (➤ 29)

The most remarkable aspects of this tiny, crumbling temple are the vast, and increasingly worn apartment towers all around. Inside incense coils hung from the ceiling evoke a spiritual mood.

Taoism and Buddhism The temple represents an eclectic mix of both the two religions, of which both have many adherents in Hong Kong. Like the Man Mo temple in Tai Po (➤ 19), although substantially larger, this place is dedicated to two Taoist deities who represent the pen and the sword. These are Man, or Man Cheong, the god of literature; and Mo, or Kuan Ti, the god of war. The statues of Man and Mo are dressed lavishly in beautifully embroidered outfits. Beside the two main statues in the temple are representations of Pao Kung, the god of justice, and Shing Wong, the god who protects this region of the city. By the door are the figures of some lesser deities, A drum and a gong are sounded whenever an offering is made to the gods. The atmosphere seems almost casual—cats wander around, fortune-tellers peer into the future using bamboo sticks, and visitors place offerings of fruit or incense sticks in the offering boxes next to the statues inside the temple.

Nearby sights Next door, to the right, is the Litt Shing Kung, or All Saints Temple. Here too, you you can see people consulting the resident soothsayers, who interpret the *chim* (numbered bamboo sticks) tipped out of bamboo pots. The room to the left of the temple was once used as a schoolroom where free education was offered to the children of poor Chinese families. Outside to the right as you leave the temple is the building across Ladder Street that was used in the 1950s movie *The World of Suzie Wong*.

CENTRAL MARKET

To appreciate fully just how different life is in Hong Kong, visit the places where people do their food shopping. Central Market sells some outrageous items, and the odor alone is exotic.

Layout This is one of Hong Kong's biggest fresh food, or "wet," markets and you should visit early, as most business is completed by mid-morning. The market is a large four-story building on the junction beftween Queen Victoria Street and Des Voeux Road. The layout is very organized, with chicken and fish on one floor, red meats on another, and fruit and vegetables on yet another. There are about 300 standholders in all, and the stock ranges from the prosaic to the peculiar—items such as salamanders and sea cucumbers.

What to look for Turtles are slaughtered to order—an especially gruesome sight—and other gory executions can be observed on the fish stands. Scrotums are a delicacy sold in the meat hall, alongside tongues, intestines, ears, and chicken feet (said to be especially good if cooked in mustard). Look for lotus root on the lower floors, a common vegetable that looks like Swiss cheese. In fall and winter the peculiar smell that rises above the other odors is not caused by a gas leak, but comes from the huge, spiky durian fruits stacked up on the fruit stands—they have a custard-like texture and a flavor that is indescribable and most definitely an acquired taste. Not for the faint-hearted.

HIGHLIGHTS

- Old-fashioned delivery bicycles on ground floor
- Fresh fish and live chickens awaiting slaughter
- Exotic green vegetables
- Strong-smelling durians
- Dried fish products
- Signs on staircases warning people not to sleep
- Hawker stands on top floor
- Beancurd product stands

INFORMATION

- D8
- Junction of Queen Victoria Street and Des Voeux Road
- Daily 7–10, 5–8
- Central
- Trams from Sheung Wan, Wan Chai and Causeway Bay
- Ferry from Tsim Sha Tsui
- None
- Free
- Exchange Square (▶ 34)
- Statue Square (▶ 36)

9

BOTANICAL & ZOOLOGICAL GARDENS

HIGHLIGHTS

- Bromeliads, air plants, and carnivorous plants
- Amazing variety of butterflies, especially in fall
- Belly-banded squirrels running free
- Black jaguar
- Orangutan families
- Tree kangaroos from central New Guinea
- Flamingos
- Local people practicing *t'ai chi chu'an*

INFORMATION

- ✚ D8
- ✉ Several entrances; from Central the most accessible gate is on Upper Albert Road
- ☎ 2530 0155
- 🕐 Daily 7AM–10PM. Aviary: 7AM–7PM
- Ⓒ Central
- 🚌 3, 12 from Connaught Road
- 🍴 Snack kiosk
- ♿ Good
- 🎟 Free
- ↔ Victoria Peak (▶ 27)
  Hong Kong Park (▶ 37)

In the middle of this urban sprawl these gardens form a quiet little haven of peace. In fall, the scents of dazzling flowers fill the air and the wings of myriad butterflies shimmer with color.

Oasis of calm This century-old complex, which once looked out over Victoria Harbour, is enclosed today by the city's towers (and bisected by a road; use the underpass to get from one part to the other). There are hundreds of species of birds, including many rare ones that breed happily in captivity. In the greenhouse are air plants, bromeliads, and insectivorous plants such as pitcher plants, Venus fly-traps, and rare butterworts. Early in the morning the gardens are full of people performing the slow exercise program know as *t'ai chi ch'uan*, which is designed to get the life forces flowing properly around the body. The zoo, though small, is surprisingly comprehensive and is also one of the world's leading centers for breeding endangered species.

Government House Opposite the gardens, on Upper Albert Road, is Government House, where Hong Kong's British governors used to live. The house was built in 1855 and was added to through the years, perhaps one of the most attractive additions being the Japanese tower and roof corners that were put up during the Occupation. Government House is closed to the public, but you can peer in through the gates or, if you are lucky, visit its gardens when they open for two days in March, when the azaleas are in bloom.

Many birds breed in the Gardens

ABERDEEN

What strikes home about crowded, lively Aberdeen, the waterborne neighborhood of sampans moored along the south side of Hong Kong Island, is the bustling life on the boats. Eating, sleeping, making a living—you see it all here.

The harbor The neighborhood of Aberdeen is one of Hong Kong's top tourist sights. In the harbor, its main attraction, many people still live on junks and sampans, rarely leaving them to set foot on dry land. Also here are several huge floating seafood restaurants, sights of interest in their own right. Free ferries make the trip out to the restaurants, and there is no obligation to eat once you get there. More fun than the ferry ride though, is to negotiate a price for a ride in a sampan with the old ladies who pilot the craft, scraping a living by taking tourists for a tour of the bay. Inland check out Aberdeen Country Park where there are walks and picnic spots.

Ap Lei Chau In the harbor is this island, best known for its junk-building. The walk across the bridge to the island offers good views of Aberdeen Harbour. Beneath the bridge are the city's dragon boats, stored away—headless —until the next Dragon Boat Festival (► 22). There is a Tin Hau temple on the island.

HIGHLIGHTS

- Traditional boatyards on Ap Lei Chau
- Fishing junks
- Floating restaurants
- Tin Hau temples
- Views of Aberdeen Harbour from Ap Lei Chau Bridge
- Old ladies chartering sampans
- Marina Club

INFORMATION

- ✠ Off map to south
- 🕐 Most restaurants are likely to close on Chinese New Year's Day
- 🍴 Floating restaurants (► 62–63)
- 🚍 7, 70 from Central Bus Terminus
- ♿ Few

Sampans in Aberdeen Harbour

11

Exchange Square

HIGHLIGHTS

- Life-sized bronze water buffalo statues
- Oversized statue of *t'ai chi ch'uan* practitioner
- Waterfront
- Land reclamation to the north
- No. 1 Exchange Square

INFORMATION

- ✚ D8
- ✉ Exchange Square, Central
- Ⓡ Central
- 🍴 Café in the Forum; also fast food available on lower floors
- ♿ Good

The best times to visit this square and the neighboring areas are when they are busy—either at lunchtime when the people who work in the area are out foraging for their lunch; or on Sunday when the Filipino maids on their day off are out picnicking with their friends.

The scene Exchange Square, designed by Hong Kong's P&T Architects in 1985, consists of several ultramodern tower blocks, including the Hong Kong Stock Exchange, set on what is, for the moment, the waterfront. The square contains some of Central's more elegantly designed structures. The towers provide shade, the waterfalls the cooling sound of water, the statuary a sense of dignity and place. It can be a chilly spot, with brisk winds seemingly always blowing straight in from the sea and channeled through the gaps between the buildings. The grand buildings are huge monoliths of smooth pink granite, quarried from one of Hong Kong's many hills.

Number 1 Take a look inside No. 1 Exchange Square. On the second floor is an exhibition gallery; the trip up the escalator takes you past another two stunning waterfalls. The overall effect of the square is very bleak. The scene is, however, consider-

Exchange Square

ably more cheerful on Sundays when the place is full of high-pitched noise and laughter and the picnickers fill every available spot.

12

LEI CHENG UK MUSEUM

Though built over an ancient Han dynasty tomb, this little museum is now surrounded by high-rise apartments occupied by thousands of Hong Kong people. This continuity between the living and the dead, spanning 2,000 years, is very moving.

Unique find The Lei Cheng Uk Museum is very modest in its appearance and layout, but it contains Hong Kong's oldest manmade structure. The tomb, built between AD 25 and 220, consists of a central domed chamber with four barrel-roofed side chambers leading from it. The entranceway was destroyed before the tomb was noticed—accidentally, in 1955, when the housing project around it was being built.

Tomb objects No human remains were found, but inscriptions on the bricks wish goodwill and peace to the region and mark the name Master Xue, perhaps the tomb's occupant or even the brickmaker. What was found were objects the deceased would need in the next life—a stove, pots and pans, a store of grain, and other essential items. The custom of buring necessities of life with deceased loved ones continues today, only nowadays videos, cash, servants, or a car deemed must-haves, and they are made out of paper and then burned at funerals and during the month of the Hungry Ghosts (▶ 22).

Lasting image The tomb is sealed and you can see it only by peering through the broken entrance porch. Nonetheless, it remains a potent image of the past that has survived in Hong Kong, and you can't help but wonder whether the Hong Kong & Shanghai Banking Corporation building will last as long.

HIGHLIGHTS

- 2,000-year-old Han Dynasty tomb with four side chambers
- Niche at back of chamber for holding funerary urn
- Display room with funerary objects
- Local park, where old men take caged birds for a walk

INFORMATION

- ✚ E2
- ✉ 41 Tonkin Street, Lei Cheng Uk Estate, Sham Shui Po
- ☎ 2386 2863
- 🕐 Mon–Sat 10–1, 2–6; Sun and some public holidays 1–6. Closed Dec 25–26 and first three days of the Chinese New Year
- 🚇 Cheung Sha Wan
- 🚌 2 from Tonkin Street to Star Ferry
- ♿ Good access to museum displays but not to tomb
- 🎟 Free

13

STATUE SQUARE

HIGHLIGHTS

- Hong Kong & Shanghai Banking Corporation Building (➤ 51)
- Old Bank of China Building
- Expatriate Filipinos gatherings on Sunday
- By-law signs written in English, Chinese, and Togalog
- Statue of Sir Thomas Jackson
- Legislative Council Building
- Cenotaphs Pier
- Chater Garden
- Interior of Mandarin Oriental Hotel (➤ 84)

INFORMATION

- ✚ E8
- ✉ Statue Square, Central
- 🚇 Central
- 🚃 Trams to Causeway Bay and Sheung Wan
- ♿ Excellent
- 🎫 Free
- ↔ Central Market (➤ 31), Star Ferry (➤ 38)

Statue Square is just one section of a whole chain of pleasant open spaces in the heart of the Central district. The space allows for amazing views of the towering landmarks of modern architecture all around you.

Colonial core Surrounded by 19th-century buildings this square once formed the heart of colonial Hong Kong Island; its northern edge opened onto the harbor. It is a far cry from that now: its only antique structure is the Legislative Council Building, previously the Supreme Court. The centerpiece was once the statue of Queen Victoria now in Victoria Park in Causeway Bay.

Surrounding architecture The square today is too built up to qualify as a green area, with its concrete pools and fountains. Much more important is the outstanding architecture around it (➤ 50). Look for Norman Foster's 1986 Hong Kong & Shanghai Banking Corporation Building (walk up to its second floor). Behind and to the east, I.M. Pei's angular 74-story Bank of China Tower (1985–90) lurches

skywards, sending out bad *chi* (➤ 50, panel). More pleasing is the old Bank of China Building (1950), guarded by two fierce stone lions. Between it and the sea is the cenotaph, memorial to the dead of two world wars and of the horrific 1989 Tiananmen Square massacre. On the other side is Chater Garden, once home to the Hong Kong Cricket Club.

Sir Thomas Jackson, architect

HONG KONG PARK

In a space-deprived Hong Kong, this modern little park is a joy, refreshing after a morning's shopping. But don't expect roses or ancient trees. Instead you'll find concrete pools for Koi fish, man-made waterfalls, and paths around the grass and flowers, all to lend a sense of harmony and balance.

Artificial paradise Hong Kong Park is a small miracle of artificiality. Its architects used what little original landscape existed and built the park into the contours of the hillside. It's fun to walk through the aviary where tree-high walkways take you cheek by bill with fascinating, brilliantly-plumaged tropical birds.

The conservatory The biggest in the world, it contains biospheres maintaining arid, humid, and just plain flashy plant environments. The utterly artificial waterfalls are beautifully designed and give a refreshing look and sound. Everywhere the plants are local and indigenous. In particular, the enormous variety of bamboos—from tiny, delicate-stemmed varieties to the huge ones used in scaffolding—are on display.

Refreshments old and new The Museum of Teaware in Flagstaff House, the oldest building in Hong Kong, deserves an afternoon. Flagstaff House is a charming piece of mid-19th-century architecture, and the exhibition of teapots and the like brings out the collector in almost everyone. After your visit, you might like to hit the happy hour, which runs between 4 and 7 in the park's bar and restaurant. Most afternoons the park is full of elegantly dressed parties posing for wedding photos, having just emerged from the marriage bureau, which is in the park.

HIGHLIGHTS

- Walk-in aviary
- Artificial waterfalls
- Conservatory
- Flagstaff House and Museum of Teaware
- Observation tower
- *Bonsai* trees in T'ai Chi Garden

INFORMATION

- E8
- Main entrancce: Supreme Court Road, Central. Nearest entrance to Museum of Teaware: Cotton Tree Drive, Central
- Museum: 2869 0690
- Park: 7AM–11PM. Museum: Tue-Sun 10–5. Closed Dec 24–25, Jan 1, and first three days of Chinese New Year
- Café/bar in park
- Admiralty
- 12, 23B, 33, 40, 103; get off at first stop in Cotton Tree Drive
- Good
- Free
- Botanical & Zoological Gardens (▶ 32)

15

STAR FERRY

The Star Ferry between Kowloon and Hong Kong Island has to be one of the world's most spectacular. For just HK$1.70 you get a panoramic view of the harbor as you dive around dredgers, speeding launches, and a rag-tag lot of other vessels.

Looking back Journey time on the Star Ferry, which has been operating since 1898, is less than ten minutes on a good day, but the views of the cityscape on both sides of the harbor are excellent. The ferry terminal on the Tsim Sha Tsui side sits beside the incongruous Hong Kong Cultural Centre (1989), with its windowless, smooth-tiled surface (▶ 51). As the ferry sets off to Hong Kong Island, you can see the long pink and black striped outlines of the Hong Kong Museum of Art (▶ 43).

Looking forward Ahead, on the island itself, the stunning architecture of the reclaimed shoreline spike the sky, dominated by the Convention and Exhibition Centre, which opened in 1988, with its twin towers of New World Harbour View and Hyatt hotels. It was built in two phases, the first by architects Mr. Ng Chun & Asociates, the second by Wong & Ouyang. Behind it is Central Plaza, at 78 stories Hong Kong's tallest office building (▶ 50). West of these buildings are the General Post Office and the striped towers of the Stock Exchange, built by Remo Riva in 1986. Behind these are the Hong Kong & Shanghai Banking Corporation Building (▶ 51), all glass and innards, and Pei's controversial Bank of China Tower (▶ 50). Try to pinpoint the various towers, each one competing with the others for advertising space, harbor views, and a postion in the *Guiness Book of Records*.

MUSEUM OF HISTORY

This gem of a Hong Kong history museum, both user-friendly and informative, is a good place to spend an hour or two, especially as the curators frequently introduce new touring shows and exhibits.

Exhibits The museum does an excellent job of turning what might be a dry set of historical records into an understandable account of the lives of the people who have inhabited Hong Kong over the years. There is a model sampan to peer into, the interior of a modest Hakka home, and costumes of the some of the peoples who migrated south from China into the New Territories. Of more recent vintage is the full-scale replica of a street in the city of Victoria, as Central was once known. The exhibits are fascinating, especially the entire medicine shop that was moved lock, stock, and barrel from its original site in Wan Chai. Other facades in the 19th-century street are of a pawn shop, opium den, print shop, teahouse, and a shop selling dried fish. Still other exhibits explore the burgeoning Hong Kong manufacturing industry of the 1950s, which produced cheap enamelware and tin toys for the world's children.

The photographic collection Even more telling are the photographs in the museum; some are of the plague that hit Hong Kong in the late 19th century, others show daily life in the streets of Hong Kong, and several much later photographs illustrate the effects the worst typhoons and landslides have had on the territory.

HIGHLIGHTS

- Early photographs
- Full-size replica of sampan
- Herbalist shop
- Interior of Eurasian family home
- *Chai mun* (ornamental plank) from temple
- Kowloon Park

INFORMATION

- ✚ F6
- ✉ 100 Chatham Road South, Tsim Sha Tsui
- ☎ 2724 9042
- 🕐 Tiue–Sat 10–6; Sun and public holidays 1–6
- 🚇 Tsim Sha Tsui
- ♿ Excellent
- 💲 Inexpensive
- ↔ Space Museum (➤ 42), Museum of Art (➤ 43)
- ❓ Audiovisual shows

Queen's Road c.1915

OCEAN PARK

Wildlife, history, scenic views, arts and crafts, and animal shows—not to mention thrilling rides—make up this park. It's a whole day's entertainment—and a crowded day at that.

HIGHLIGHTS

- Atoll reef aquarium
- Shark aquarium
- Butterfly house
- Middle Kingdom
- Ocean Theatre animal shows
- Raging River flume ride
- Aviary
- Bird shows at bird theater
- Dragon Ride

INFORMATION

- ✚ Off map to south
- ✉ Aberdeen, Hong Kong
- ☎ 2837 8888 or 2555 3554
- ◷ Daily 10–6
- ⅊ Several fast-food eateries inside
- ⊟ Ocean Park Citibus leaves from Exchange Square Bus Terminus every half hour
- ⚒ Excellent
- ⚑ Expensive
- ❓ Height restrictions on some rides

Dolphin ride

Thrills galore There is so much to see and do at this park that it takes a little doing to figure out a plan. So start by finding out the times and locations of the animal shows; then plan the rest of your day around them. The rides really are stomach-turning, the creatures in the aquarium scary, and the animal and plant exhibits well-displayed and well-maintained. Don't miss the Raging River breathtaking flume ride.

Aerial view Most fun of all, perhaps, is the cable-car trip into the place. You dangle in a fragile little car, stopping and starting for no apparent reason as the wind whistles around and under you, with the sea gently boiling below. And to come out of the park you take a four-section, 250-yard-long escalator ride. Try to avoid weekends, when the place gets very crowded, and note there are minimum height restrictions on some rides.

TEMPLE STREET

At about 7PM each night, racks sprout on either side of this street and are hung with T-shirts, lingerie, jeans, and other goodies. Earlier in the day, stands do a brisk trade in jade.

After dark The market is full of bargains on silk shirts, leather items, and bric-a-brac, as well as jeans and T-shirts. Nothing on sale is really indigenous as locals rather than the tourists are the market. After about 7:30PM the street is closed to traffic, and at the crossroads in the middle of the market, two fresh-fish restaurants set up their tables. Their counters, also out in the street, contain all manner of wriggling things that you can pick out to be cooked for your dinner.

Jade for sale At the end of the street, near the junction of Battery and Kansu streets under a overpass, is the jade market. Here, until they close up at about 3PM, hundreds of stands sell all kinds of jade, which comes in many colors besides the popular green—from white through to purple. Locals spend the afternoon bargaining over prices, which range from inexpensive to a king's ransom. Unless you know what you are doing, this is not the place to make a major investment.

Still more stands In adjoining streets are vegetable and fruit stands, stores selling fabrics and traditional red-embroidered Chinese wedding outfits, and many Chinese medicine stores. If you are lucky, you may catch a Chinese opera performance, sung in Cantonese, on a makeshift stage of bamboo and canvas.

Tradition As you walk through the market, look for people playing the age-old game of mahjong in the backs of stores or set up in corners.

HIGHLIGHTS

- Fresh fish set out on stands
- Fortune-tellers
- Chinese medicine shops
- Shops selling traditional Chinese wedding clothes
- Jade market
- Yau Ma Tei Typhoon Shelter, to the west
- Racks of T-shirts
- Exotic vegetables in vegetable market

INFORMATION

- ✚ F5–6
- ✉ Temple Street, Kansu Street, Reclamation Street, Kowloon
- 🕐 Jade market: 10–4. Temple Street market: 8AM–11PM. Vegetable market: early morning and early evening
- 🍴 Seafood restaurants and hawker center in Temple Street
- 🚇 Jordan
- ♿ Good
- 🎫 Free
- ↔ Lei Cheng Uk Museum (➤ 35)

SPACE MUSEUM

HIGHLIGHTS

- Omnimax Theatre
- Moon rocks
- *Mercury space capsule*
- Hall of Space Science
- Solar telescope
- Planetarium show
- Hall of Astronomy

INFORMATION

- ✚ F7
- ✉ 10 Salisbury Road (next to the Hong Kong Cultural Centre, Tsim Sha Tsui
- ☎ 2721 0226
- 🕐 Mon, Wed–Fri noon –8:45PM (Fri 9:45PM); Sat, Sun 10 –8:45PM
- 🚇 Tsim Sha Tsui
- 🚌 Tsim Sha Tsui bus station
- ⛴ Star Ferry to Central and Wan Chai
- ♿ Excellent
- 💰 Expensive
- ↔ Hong Kong Science Museum (▶ 58)
- ❓ Children under three are not allowed in the Omnimax

*This museum, which has one of the largest and most advanced planetariums in the world, is fascinating for kids of all ages, with plenty of hands-on exhibits, a genuine **Mercury** space capsule, and daily Omnimax and Space Theatre shows.*

Layout and Omnimax The museum's oval, pink building, built in 1980 by the Architectural Services Department, is in itself stunning. Inside are three exhibitions: the Hall of Astronomy, the Hall of Space Science, and the most popular, the Omnimax Theatre. If you haven't seen an Omnimax movie before, then seize the chance here. You sit back in tilted seats and gaze ahead and up at a screen that covers most of the ceiling and front wall. If you get at all queasy at thrill rides at amusement parks, close your eyes during the parts where someone jumps out of an airplane or travels around in a roller coaster—these are very realistic.

Exhibition Halls The Space Science Exhibition includes bits of moon rock, manned spaced flight, the actual *Mercury* space capsule piloted by Scott Carpenter in 1962, future space programs, and plenty more. In the Museum of Astronomy, there is a solar telescope where you can look directly at the sun. Did you know that it was ancient Chinese astronomers who were the first to spot Halley's Comet and the first to chart the movements of the stars?

Gravity chair, with astronaut in action shown behind

MUSEUM OF ART

A beautifully laid-out series of galleries here contain displays of exquisite Chinese calligraphy and painting, both traditional and modern, many stunning ancient artifacts, and a collection of jade, ivory, and pottery.

Chinese antiquities Opened in 1989, next door to the Hong Kong Cultural Centre complex, the museum has six galleries, four containing Chinese antiquities, local artists' work, and pictures of historical note as well as artistic worth. The thousands of exhibits in the Chinese antiquities section range from rhino-horn cups to burial goods and tomb adornments; of particular interest are two large Tang Dynasty (AD 618–906) tomb guardians in the form of mythical beasts. The jade and ivory carvings in the Decorative Arts gallery are especially lovely.

Art galleries The best gallery is the one containing old pictures and prints of Hong Kong. It is hard to believe that the sandy beaches and jungle-filled hills could have become such a different kind of jungle in so short a space of time. The painting of the city of Victoria (as the built-up part of Hong Kong was called) is a revelation of just how far the colony has come since the early 19th century.

Modern art The works in the contemporary art gallery are divided into decades, and it is particularly interesting to see the development of local art since the 1950s. There is also a collection of calligraphy and Chinese paintings, and a special gallery for international exhibitions. Between galleries, leather armchairs facing the enormous corridor windows allow you to enjoy the wonderful harbor vista.

HIGHLIGHTS

- Han Dynasty pottery watch-tower
- Tang Dynasty tomb guardians
- Translucent rhino-horn cups
- Description of Quing kiln
- Painting of city of Victoria (1854)
- Painting of Wyndham Street
- *The Baptism* in contemporary art gallery
- Models of merchant boats and sea-going junk
- Model of Guangzhou
- Lithograph of Hong Kong Harbour

INFORMATION

- ✚ F7
- ✉ 10 Sailsbury Road (next door to the Hong Kong Cultural Centre, Tsim Sha Tsui
- ☎ 2721 0116
- 🕐 Fri–Wed 10–6. Closed some public holidays
- 🍴 Café within Cultural Centre complex
- Ⓠ Tsim Sha Tsui
- 🚌 Tsim Sha Tsui bus station
- ⛴ Star Ferry to Wan Chai and Central
- ♿ Excellent
- 💲 Expensive
- ↔ Star Ferry (▶ 38)

PAK TAI TEMPLE

In the back halls of this elderly temple you can see craftsmen working at one of the most unusual trades you may ever come across—the making of the modern, paper equivalents of prehistoric grave goods.

HIGHLIGHTS

- Roof decorations
- Statue of Pak Tai
- Burial offerings
- Nearby Hung Sheng Temple (Queen's Road East) and Tai Wong Street bird market
- Nearby Wan Chai Post Office (Queen's Road East; opened 1915)

INFORMATION

- F9
- Lung On Street, off Queen's Road East, Wan Chai
- Wan Chai
- 260,15 from Central; get off at Wan Chai Market
- None
- Free, but donations welcome
- Hong Kong Park, Flagstaff House and Museum of Teaware (➤ 37) Hung Sheng Temple (➤ 53)

Pak Tai Built in the 1860s, the temple is dedicated to Pak Tai, the military protector whose job is to maintain peace. His representation in this temple is a 17th-century copper statue seated on a throne. The face is blackened, the hair real, and its clothing sumptuously embroidered. Around it are arranged four figures that represent warriors and scholars.

Worship Like all Taoist temples, this one has no set service times. People come at any time to pray, make an offering, or to seek help regarding their future from soothsayers who use the bamboo sticks called *chim*. The air is full of the heady mixture of incense and the perfume of fruit and flowers left by worshippers. You can sometimes smell paper burning—the paper is money, offered essentially as a bribe to the gods.

Model business If ever there is an insight into the money-oriented greed of Hong Kong, it is a Pak Tai. In the side room of the temple, men sit making models of everything the recently deceased might need in the afterlife. Rolls Royces, servants, houses, suites of furniture, VCRs, and money are all painstakingly made out of paper and thin strips of bamboo. The models are collected together and displayed at the funeral as an indication of the person's prestige, then burned so that they can accompany the deceased on his or her journey to heaven. It's proof that in Hong Kong, if you didn't have money in this life, people still pray that you will get it in your next life.

22

TEN THOUSAND BUDDHAS TEMPLE

A half-hour train ride out of Hong Kong brings you to this striking temple set on a hillside overlooking the apartments, housing projects, and towers of the satellite town of Sha Tin.

Bountiful Buddhas To reach the temple, take the train to Sha Tin and follow the signs. You must then climb 431 steps up the hillside. Known locally as Man Fat Sze Temple, this Buddhist shrine has, since it was built in the 1950s, become known as the Ten Thousand Buddhas Temple because of the many small statues that decorate it, the donations of grateful worshippers over the years. The statues are all different—some black, some covered in gold leaf—and each Buddha strikes a different pose.

Panoramas and pagodas From the edge of the courtyard there are magnificent views over Sha Tin. The courtyard houses a tiered pagoda and the statues of some of Buddha's followers. Higher up is another set of four temples, one containing Hong Kong's second-tallest Buddha statue, another the embalmed, gilded remains of Yuet Kai, who founded the Man Fat Sze monastery.

HIGHLIGHTS

- Thousands of small statues of Buddha
- Tallest standing Buddha statue in Hong Kong
- Embalmed and gilded body of monastery's founder
- Statues of Buddha's followers
- Views over Sha Tin
- 400-odd steps up to monastery
- Views of Amah Rock

INFORMATION

- ✚ Off map to north
- ✉ Close to Pai Tau Street, Sha Tin, New Territories
- 🕐 Daily 8–6. Particularly busy around Chinese New Year
- 🚇 Sha Tin
- ♿ None
- 🎫 Free, but donations welcome

Courtyard of the Ten Thousand Buddhas Temple

23

WONG TAI SIN TEMPLE

HIGHLIGHTS

- Main altar including painting of Wong Tai Sin
- Garden of Nine Dragon Wall
- Fortune-telling arcade
- Clinic Block
- Stands outside selling windmills and hell money
- Chinese gardens at rear of complex
- Side altar in main temple dedicated to monkey god
- Incinerators for burning offerings

INFORMATION

✚ H1

✉ Wong Tai Sin Estate; follow signs from MTR station

☎ Information hotline: 2802 0200

🕐 Daily 7–5. Main temple is not always accessible

🚇 Wong Tai Sin

♿ Good

🎟 Free, but donations welcome

If temples were stores, then Wong Tai Sin Temple would be a supermarket. During Chinese New Year, you risk having your hair set on fire by hundreds of devotees waving joss sticks as they whirl from one deity to the next.

Wong Tai Sin This large Taoist temple, built in 1973 in Chinese style and situated among high-rise residential complexes, is dedicated to Wong Tai Sin, an ex-shepherd who was taught how to cure all ills by a passing deity. In modern-day Hong Kong, Wong Tai Sin is a very popular god, as he is in charge of the fortunes of gamblers. He can also be sought out by those who are ill or worried about their health, and by people asking for help in business matters.

Temple interior The temple complex is vast, almost stadium-sized, composed not just of the main temple, where Wong Tai Sin is represented by a painting rather than a statue, but also by turtle ponds, libraries, medicine halls, and what is almost a small shopping center of fortune-tellers. The temple is built to represent the five geomantic elements of gold, wood, water, fire, and earth. In the Yue Heung Shrine are fire and earth; gold is represented in the Bronze Luen Pavilion where the portrait of Wong Tai Sin is kept; and the Library Hall and water fountain represent wood and water respectively.

Philosophy The Temple also caters to those who venerate Confucius, represented in the Confucius Hall, while Buddhists come here to worship the Buddhist goddess of mercy, Kuan Yin, in the Three Saints Hall alongside Kwan Ti, and the eight immortals.

AW BOON HAW GARDENS

There is something poignant about this rather sad, crumbling place, affectionately known as Tiger Balm Gardens. The paint is faded, the concrete cracked, and the statues have disappeared. As a monument to the transience of wealth and power, these gardens are second to none.

Visions of hell Tiger Balm Gardens, as they are more generally known, were built in 1935 by the millionaire philanthropist Aw Boon Haw, who made his fortune from Tiger Balm ointment, still rubbed into sore joints throughout Hong Kong and Southeast Asia. Concrete statues of figures in Chinese mythology and victims being tortured in hell fill the gardens, although the concrete sea lions stuck for ever in a concrete sea are perhaps most worthy of pity. At the very back of the garden, a bas-relief concrete panel shows the horrors that befall those who maltreat their elders, forcibly adopt children, commit adultery, or otherwise behave badly. The ninth degree of hell looks the worst, although what the goat is doing is a bit of a mystery; in the eighth level sinners are run over by a 1940s truck.

Other sights The gardens' pagoda is said to have cost HK$1 million in 1930; the view from the top is very good. There are also little grottoes, caves with Chinese myths depicted inside, and a model of the jade bridge over which the righteous walk to their next incarnation. The towering apartment houses that surround the gardens make you wonder if some of the indignities of hell aren't already with us.

HIGHLIGHTS

- The villa
- Phoenix, dragon, and lion in frieze behind villa
- Mazes of steps and grottoes
- Statues of Buddha explaining stages of enlightenment
- Ten Courts of Hell
- Truck in eighth level of Hell
- Jade bridge through which good people are reincarnated into a rich family
- Cactus plants near waterfall

INFORMATION

- ✚ H9
- ✉ Tai Hang Road, Happy Valley
- 🕐 Daily 9:30–4
- 🚇 Causeway Bay
- 🚌 11 from Central Bus Terminal
- ♿ None
- 🎟 Free

Aw Boon Haw Gardens

25

STANLEY

HIGHLIGHTS

- Views from bus to Stanley
- Tin Hau Temple
- Stanley Beach
- St. Stephen's Beach
- Stanley Military Cemetery
- Stanley market
- Kuan Yin Temple

INFORMATION

- Off map to south
- Market: 10:30–9.
  Temple: 6–6
- Restaurants and bar food in Stanley Main Street
- 6, 260 from Central Bus Terminus
- Excellent
- Tours (➤ 19)

The most stunning thing about visiting Stanley, in the south of Hong Kong Island, is the scenic and at times precarious journey there. Get an upstairs seat on the double-decker bus—the ride is as good as any at Ocean Park.

Temples Most visitors come to Stanley Village for its market, but it has many other attractions. Close to the market is the Tin Hau Temple, first built on this spot in the early 1700s. The bell and drum are said to have belonged to a famous pirate, Cheung Po-Tsai. The bell was cast in 1767, and it is thought that the pirate used it to send messages to his ships. The temple also contains the skin of a tiger, shot in Stanley in 1942. During the Japanese invasion the villagers took refuge inside the temple, and although the building was hit twice, neither bomb exploded. Further along the road is a second temple, dedicated to Kuan Yin, the goddess of mercy. Claims have been made that the 20-foot statue of the goddess has moved. Nowadays Stanley is a commuter town, popular with expatriate workers.

Beaches and the market The beach at Stanley is a good one, and a short bus ride farther along takes you to St. Stephen's Beach, where there is a graveyard for all the soldiers who have died in Hong Kong since Britain claimed the island as a colony. Although now rather touristy, the famous market is quite good, with linen shops as well as stands selling clothes made in other Asian countries.

Stanley market

HONG KONG's *best*

ARCHITECTURE

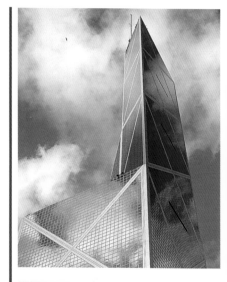

Bank of China Tower

See Top 25 Sights for
EXCHANGE SQUARE (▶ 34)

Geomancers

Almost all building that goes on in Hong Kong is overseen by a *feng shui* (literally "wind and water") master, someone who knows how the life force, or *chi*, moves around the planet's surface. Sharp angles send out bad *chi*, while strategically placed water and mirrors can enhance good *chi* by allowing it to flow smoothly and not get trapped in corners. The master may have much to say about the building's structure; he also studies the site and will decide an auspicious day for starting work.

BANK OF CHINA TOWER

Designed by the Chinese-American architect, I. M. Pei and built between 1985 and 1990, this 984-foot-high, 70-story tower dominates the Hong Kong skyline. The building soars upwards in a series of triangles towards a prism at the top. Amazingly, it is built with no internal supporting columns. The entrance hall has barreled vaults in the style of a Ming Dynasty tomb—a typically Hong Kong mixture of the ultramodern and the historic. It is world famous for its bad *chi* owing to the use of sharp angles creating a sinister shape.

➕ E8   ✉ No 1 Garden Road, Central   🕐 Mon–Fri 9–5   🚇 Central   🆓 Free

CENTRAL PLAZA

Completed in 1992, Central Plaza is Hong Kong's tallest building at 78 stories and 1,227 feet (counting the spire). Majestic both inside and out, it incorporates a huge public space, in the form of a piazza at ground level and a through walkway on the first level. The whole mood is one of brooding neoclassical grandeur, with its vast lobby containing two-story palm trees and some terrific artwork. The architects were Dennis Lau and Ng Chun Man.

➕ F8   ✉ Harbour Road, Wan Chai   🚇 Wan Chai   🆓 Free

HONG KONG & SHANGHAI BANKING CORPORATION BUILDING

This 1985 building, designed by Britain's Sir Norman Foster and prefabricated in several different continents at a cost of over US$1 billion, looks as if it's been turned inside out. The supporting structures appear on the outside, all mechanical parts are exposed, and many walls are glass. A geomancer decided the alignment and angles of the escalators.

➕ E8   ✉ Des Voeux Road and Statue Square, Central   🚇 Central
🚌 Free

HONG KONG CONVENTION & EXHIBITION CENTRE

Built on reclaimed land and opened in 1988 (▶ 38), this massive complex looks bland when approached from the harbor, despite the fact that its towers contain two of the island's most prestigious hotels—the Renaissance Harbour View and the Grand Hyatt—plus some 2,153 square yards of exhibition space. On the harbor side of the exhibition hall is a seven-story plate-glass window. Escalators go alongside it up to the seventh floor, giving great harbor views.

➕ F8   ✉ 1 Convention Avenue, Wan Chai   ☎ 2582 8888
🚇 Wan Chai   🚌 Free

HONG KONG CULTURAL CENTRE

Designed by the government's architectural services department in 1989, this is one of Hong Kong's most controversial buildings. It has a huge sloping roof that is matched by the dome of the nearby Space Museum, and is uniformly pink. The building is also windowless—rather odd as it would have one of the most dynamic views in the world. Inside, it is all very modern, especially the sparse auditoriums with their apparently unsupported balconies. At the rear is a harborfront walkway.

➕ F7   ✉ Salisbury Road, Tsim Sha Tsui
☎ 2734 20109   🚇 Tsim Sha Tsui
🚌 Free

THE WHAMPOA

The Whampoa, completed in 1991, may not have the statistics of other buildings here, but it must be one of the few ship-shaped concrete developments in the world and looks as if it is about to set sail. Built by Robert Lam into the space once occupied by a dry dock, it is a shopping center—with movie theaters and ice rink.

➕ G5   ✉ Sung King Street, Hung Hom   🚌 Bus 6 from Hanlow Road or taxi from Tsim Sha Tsui MTR   🚌 Free

---

Feng shui in practice

When the Conrad Hotel was redesigned in 1997, coins were buried beneath the floor of the downstairs lobby, itself in the shape of a Chinese coin. The carp and lily paintings on the walls of the hotel lobby represent pools of water, so bring in good *chi* and they hold it there. At the Excelsior Hotel, built in 1973, the Chinese restaurant was designed with temporary moving partitions so that the series of small rooms could periodically be opened up into a large loop, allowing a good flow of *chi* through the restaurant.

Hong Kong Convention and Exhibition Centre

GREEN SPACES

See Top 25 Sights for
HONG KONG PARK (▶ 37)
VICTORIA PEAK (▶ 27)

CHEUNG CHAU
Cheung Chau has two good beaches, lots of seafood restaurants, some interesting temples, caves, windsurfing equipment and bicycles for rent, good walks, no traffic, and an annual bun festival.

Cheung Chau Island

🕐 Hourly ferries start around 6:30AM. Last ferry returns around 11:30PM 🚢 Outlying Islands Pier, Central 🚶 Moderate

KOWLOON PARK
(▶ 59)

LAMMA ISLAND
Great beaches, plenty of good seafood restaurants, places to walk, and no cars. Even the power station and a huge quarry do not spoil a great day out. The nicest beach is at Mo Tat Wan.
🕐 Ferries run approx 7AM–10:30PM 🚢 Outlying Islands Pier, Central 🚶 Moderate; double on weekends

PENG CHAU
This tiny island is densely populated, with a crowded village, a market, and some cottage industries. Sewage can make it undesirable to swim on the east side of the island.
🕐 Ferries start around 7AM and run hourly. Last ferry returns around 11:30PM 🍴 Cafés 🚢 Outlying Islands Pier, Central 🚶 Moderate; double on weekends

TAI TAM COUNTRY PARK
An excellent country park, perfect when the crowds begin to oppress you. You can walk along the coast and around a reservoir, past World War II bunkers and fortified gun emplacements. Bring sturdy shoes and something to drink if you intend to walk for long.
➕ J8–K8/9/10 🚇 Wan Chai MTR, then minibus 16M or 🚌 6 from Exchange Square to Hong Kong Cricket Club, then walk past gas station and take first left up steps

VICTORIA PARK
This relatively enormous patch of green is used to its limits, including its sports fields, pool, and pleasant green walks. Early morning *t'ai chi ch'uan* takes place and many events are staged here.
➕ G8–H8 ✉ Causeway Bay, Hong Kong Island 🚊 Tram from Wan Chai or Central (look for one labeled "Causeway Bay") 🎫 Free

Country parks
Hong Kong Island has five country parks, areas of protected countryside, all linked together along the 31-mile Hong Kong Trail, a well-laid out footpath. Each park has barbecue sites and other facilities, but they do get very crowded on weekends. However, if you venture any distance along the trail, you soon leave the crowds behind. The most accessible park is probably Pok Fu Lam Country Park, which can be reached on foot from the Peak or by the No. 15 bus from Central.

TEMPLES

LU PAN TEMPLE

Usually empty and quiet, this is the only temple in Hong Kong dedicated to Lu Pan, the master builder who repaired the pillars of heaven. His festival is celebrated by construction workers. The temple has elaborate roof ceramics and carvings above the door.

🕂 B8   ✉ Li Po Lung Path, off Belcher's Street, Kennedy Town
🕙 Daily 8–7   🚌 3 from Rumsey Steet, Central   🎫 Free

MAN MO TEMPLE, TAI PO (► 19)

HUNG SHENG TEMPLE

This temple, built quite a way back into the rock-face behind it, is dedicated to the scholar Hung Sheng, who was able to foretell the weather. Several elderly fortune-tellers have set up little shrines around it.

🕂 F9   ✉ 131 Queen's Road East, Wan Chai   🕙 Daily 8–6
🚇 Wan Chai   🎫 Free

TIN HAU TEMPLE, CAUSEWAY BAY

Dedicated to Tin Hau, the goddess who protects seafarers, this is one of many temples scattered along Hong Kong's coastline. The temple, perched on a rock above the road, is about 200 years old, although it has been renovated.

🕂 H8   ✉ Tin Hau Street, Causeway Bay   🕙 Daily 8–6   🚇 Tin Hau
🎫 Free

TIN HAU TEMPLE, KOWLOON

Kowloon's temple of the goddess of the sea and seafarers, after which Temple Street is named, is one of Kowloon's oldest. Once it looked out to the sea, now several blocks away.

🕂 F5   ✉ Market Street, Kowloon   🕙 Daily 8–6   🚇 Jordan
🎫 Free

TIN HAU TEMPLE, REPULSE BAY

Yet another Tin Hau temple dedicated to the goddess of fisherfolk, this one has a longevity bridge in front of it; crossing it is said to add three years to your life.

✉ Repulse Bay Beach   🕙 Daily 8–6   🚌 6, 61 from Central Bus Terminus   🎫 Free

Other places of worship

Many religions are practiced in Hong Kong beside Taoism and Buddhism. The colony has a synagogue and two mosques as well as many churches. The two most prominent are the Roman Catholic cathedral, built in 1880 by Portuguese Catholics from Macau, and the Anglican St. John's Cathedral in Garden Road, built in 1847. Both are open to the public and well worth a visit, if only for the sense of what life must have been like in 19th-century Hong Kong.

Roof decoration of Wong Tai Sin Temple

MARKETS

Bird markets

Songbirds have always played an important part in Hong Kong's social life. Keeping the birds is a male activity, and an elderly man taking his bird for a walk is a common sight in parks. Regularly there are regular impromptu bird-song competitions, when a judge listens to the songs of birds in different cages, and large sums of money are wagered on which bird will win the prize. The bird cages are little works of art in themselves, often carved out of mahogany or bamboo.

See Top 25 Sights for
JADE MARKET (► 41)
STANLEY MARKET (► 48)
TEMPLE STREET NIGHT MARKET (► 41)

APLIU STREET
Tour buses rarely include this thoroughly Chinese market area in their itineraries. It sells clothes, inexpensive CDs, and sundry items. The Golden Shopping Centre (► 73) is in the vicinity.
➕ E3 ✉ Apliu Street, Sham Shui Po, Kowloon ⏰ Daily mid-morning–late 🚇 Sham Shui Po

BIRD MARKET
This market is dedicated to the sale of songbirds and all the associated paraphernalia, from bird seed to cages. Local bird fanciers prefer the tiny birds, but you will also find more exotic creatures such as parrots and mynahs. Look for cages of crickets, which are fed to the birds with chopsticks.
➕ F3 ✉ Yuen Po Street, Mong Kok ⏰ Daily Daily 7AM–8PM 🚇 Mong Kok

Bird market

FA YUEN STREET
Two blocks heaving with local color. There are some amazing bargains in inexpensive clothes.
➕ F3 ✉ Prince Edward MTR ⏰ Daily 10AM–late

FLOWER MARKET
A whole street is given over to potted-plant and

cut-flower stalls. Look for the carnivorous pitcher plants and beautiful but very expensive bonsai. Silk flowers are also sold.

➕ F3 ✉ Flower Market Road, Kowloon ⏰ Daily 9–6
🚇 Prince Edward

Card players near Jade Market

JARDINE'S BAZAAR
This is one of Hong Kong's oldest street markets, full of food stores, good shops selling clothes and handbags, and excellent bargains in inexpensive clothes.

➕ G8 ✉ Jardine's Bazaar and Jardine's Crescent, Causeway Bay
⏰ Daily mid-morning–late 🚇 Causeway Bay

LADIES' MARKET
This market easily rivals Temple Street, and although once solely dedicated to women's clothes, it now has bargains for everyone, including printed T-shirts, belts, inexpensive jeans, and watches. It covers about four blocks of densest Mong Kok, so you have to love crowds to shop here.

➕ F4 ✉ Tung Choi Street, Mong Kok ⏰ Daily noon–10
🚇 Mong Kok

LI YUEN STREET EAST AND WEST
A clothes, handbag, fabric, and accessories market, one of Hong Kong's oldest, with some excellent bargains, particularly in leather goods. It could be combined with the factory outlets in the Pedder Building (► 77).

➕ D8 ✉ Off Queen's Road Central, Central ⏰ Daily noon–late
🚇 Central

MARBLE ROAD MARKET
This busy working local market sells fresh produce and there are bargains in T-shirts and clothes. A fish market is nearby.

➕ J7 ✉ Marble Road, North Point ⏰ Daily noon–late 🚋 Tram from Causeway Bay, Wan Chai or Central

UPPER LASCAR ROW
A flea market set alongside more expensive stores and selling the same kind of bric-a-brac, records, and curios along with the occasional antique.

➕ D8 ✉ Off Queen's Road West, Sheung Wan ⏰ Daily 11–6
🚇 Sheung Wan

WESTERN MARKET
Gift items, crafts, paintings, fabrics, and restaurants.

➕ D7 ✉ New Market Street, Sheung Wan ⏰ Daily 10 –7
🚇 Sheung Wan

Flower markets

Hong Kong's several markets dedicated to flowers sell mostly cut flowers and silk ones. Around Chinese New Year additional flower markets spring up all around—a particularly big one is held in Victoria Park. Families go there to buy kumquat trees, orange trees, and plum-blossom branches to decorate their homes. Particularly favored at this time are exquisitely perfumed daffodils and gladioli.

SHOPPING CENTERS

Pacific Place

Pacific Place is part of a vast linked chain of shopping malls that spreads out around Admiralty MTR station. Built around a very tall atrium, decorated in granite pink, chrome, and glass, it is visually captivating as well as a great place to shop. Most stores sell clothes, but you will also find with three hotels, restaurants, fast-food joints, a huge branch of Marks & Spencer, a supermarket, three movie theaters, and a Seibu Japanese department store. The main concourse is often the venue for free concerts.

Admiralty Building

CITYPLAZA I AND II

Try this center if you want to see one that is used by lots of locals and is rarely visited by tourists. It has stores with fixed prices, and its two skating rinks—roller and ice—have attracted childrenswear and toy stores. There are also men's and women's clothes stores.

➕ K8   ✉ 1111 King's Road, Taikoo Shing   🕐 Daily 9–8   🚇 Tai Koo

THE LANDMARK

A very exclusive mall with all the big-name designer labels and prices to match. There are numerous cafés and a huge atrium with an impressive fountain, where free concerts are frequently given. Another attraction is the musical clock, ornamented with figures from the Chinese zodiac.

➕ D8   ✉ Des Voeux Road and Pedder Street, Central   🕐 Daily 9–8   🚇 Central

NEW WORLD CENTRE

Slightly more elegant and rarefied than the other malls, but a bit gloomy and architecturally unimpressive, the New World Centre has lots of stores selling silks and jade, as well as some excellent rosewood and lacquer furniture stores. Try the Regalia Art Treasures store (▶ 71).

➕ F7   ✉ Salisbury Road, Tsim Sha Tsui   🕐 Daily 9–8   🚇 Tsim Sha Tsui

OCEAN TERMINAL

This mega mall stretches along the length of Canton Road and seems to go on forever. It has a wide variety of stores ranging from designer fashion to interesting furniture and fabric stores.

➕ F6   ✉ Canton Road, Tsim Sha Tsui   🕐 Daily 9–8   🚇 Tsim Sha Tsui

PACIFIC PLACE

You could live and die in this shopping center without ever having to leave. (▶ panel).

➕ E8   ✉ 88 Queensway, Central   🕐 Daily 9–8   🚇 Admiralty

PINOY WORLD

This shopping center is dedicated to all things Filipino, with shops, restaurants, and live-music performances. Hong Kong has about 130,000 Filipino workers, who all get the day off

Pacific Place

on Sunday and who congregate around the open spaces of Central. This shopping complex offers a variety of products not easily found elsewhere, including delicacies and crafts from the Philippines as well as services such as shipping agents and employment agencies.

🚩 G4 ✉ Ma Tau Wai Road, Kowloon 🕐 Daily 9–8 🚌 5A from Tsim Sha Tsui Star Ferry

SHUN TAK CENTRE

The biggest mall in the western end of the island, this is built around a residential hotel, offices, and the ferry terminal to Macau. It has large open spaces with cafés, food stands, lots of local chain stores, and some interesting clothes and leather shops. Worth popping into on a trip to Western Market—it's almost directly opposite—for its air-conditioning and refreshments as well as the stores.

🚩 D7 ✉ 200 Connaught Road, Sheung Wan 🕐 Daily 9–8
🚇 Sheung Wan

TIMES SQUARE

In this space-age super mall, each floor is dedicated to a certain type of product—all the computer merchandise is on one floor, the women's clothes are on another, and so on. It is in the excellent shopping area of Causeway Bay with other plazas close by as well as several Japanese department stores and Chinese products stores, so if you have time to visit only one shopping area, choose this one. Stay away on weekends, when vast crowds flood in.

🚩 G8 ✉ Matheson Street, Causeway Bay 🕐 Daily 9–8
🚇 Causeway Bay

Harbour City

The Harbour City complex in Tsim Sha Tsui is one of the world's longest shopping complexes and includes Ocean Centre, Ocean Galleries, a few hotels, and Ocean Terminal. If you can't find what you want here, it probably doesn't exist.

FOR KIDS

See Top 25 Sights for
OCEAN PARK (➤ 40)

More ideas

Like the rest of us, children enjoy spending money, and Hong Kong is a good place to blow the contents of a piggy bank. Older kids may go for the designer sportswear—fake and the real thing—found in the side streets of Mong Kok. Ocean Terminal has an enormous Toys'R'Us, and hundreds of stores around Nathan Road sell electronic toys and games.

CITY PLAZA II ICE PALACE AND ROLLERWORLD

This shopping center houses two skating rinks—ice and roller. The admission price includes skate rental and two hours' skating. In the same building is Fourseas Bowling Centre.

🚇 K8 ✉ Tai Koo Shing, Hong Kong Island. 🍴 Cafés 🚇 Tai Koo Shing

Ice Palace: ☎ 2885 6697 🕐 Daily 7AM–10PM 💰 Moderate
Rollerworld: ☎ 2567 0391 🕐 Daily 9–9 💰 Moderate
Fourseas Bowling Centre: ☎ 2567 0763 🕐 Daily 9:30am–1AM
💰 Moderate

DRAGON SHOPPING CENTRE

The main attraction of this shopping center, opened in 1996, is the rollercoaster ride that whizzes about inside the building. There is also a skating rink and a video arcade. You can get in some serious shopping while the kids have fun.

🚇 E2 ✉ Yen Chow Street, Sham Shui Po ☎ 2360 0982
🕐 Daily 11–10 🚇 Sham Shui Po MTR 💰 Ride: inexpensive

HONG KONG SCIENCE MUSEUM

In this multi-level hands-on museum, kids and science freaks will defintely get a kick out of the zany, yet eductional, interactive exhibits on permanent display—some 500 in all, covering computers, robotics, energy, physics, transportation, communications, and much more. Over half are interactive.

🚇 F6 ✉ 2 Science Museum Road, Tsim Sha Tsui ☎ 2732 3231
🕐 Tue–Fri 1–9; Sat–Sun 10–9 🚌 6 from Hanlow Road or taxi from Tsim Sha Tsui MTR 💰 Moderate

POK FU LAM PUBLIC RIDING SCHOOL

This riding school on the southwest of the Island provides lessons for all abilities. Be sure to telephone in advance.

🚇 C10 ✉ 75 Reservoir Road, Pok Fu Lam
☎ 2551 0030 🕐 Sep–Jun. Tue–Sun
💰 Moderate

POLICE MUSEUM (➤ 59)

REPULSE BAY

The pretty beach here gets very crowded on public holidays and on weekends, but there is a temple (➤ 53) and a modern shopping arcade to visit when the heat gets too much.

🚌 6, 61 from Central Bus Terminus 💰 Free

Repulse Bay

WHAT'S FREE

> **See Top 25 Sights for**
> **AW BOON HAW GARDENS (► 47)**
> **BOTANICAL GARDENS (► 32)**

CITY HALL COMPLEX
The City Hall complex has a garden where you can watch wedding parties posing for photos, plus several libraries containing rare material on microfilm, back copies of newspapers, and a wealth of material on local culture and issues. Bring your passport for ID.
➕ E8 ✉ Edinburgh Place, Central ☎ 9221 2840 🕓 Libraries: Mon–Thu 10–7; Fri 10–9; Sat 10–5; Sun 10–1 🚇 Central 🚢 Star Ferry

LAW UK FOLK MUSEUM
A 200-year-old house furnished in Hakka style. Displays show how Hakka farmers lived complete with furniture and farm tools.
➕ M10 ✉ 14 Kut Shing Street, Chai Wan ☎ 2896 7006 🕓 Tue–Sat 10–1, 2–6; Sun and holidays 1–6. Closed some holidays 🚇 Chai Wan

CHINESE UNIVERSITY OF HONG KONG ART GALLERY
This collection of Chinese art includes over 1,000 paintings and pieces of calligraphy, bronze seals from the Han Dynasty (AD 25–220), and over 400 jade flower carvings.
➕ Off map to north ✉ Chinese University, Sha Tin ☎ 2609 7416 🕓 Mon–Sat 10–4:45; Sun 12:30–5:30. Closed some holidays 🚇 University, then shuttle bus

KOWLOON PARK
For a short wander or a rest in between shopping trips, try this little oasis. There's a statue collection, an aviary, a children's playground, some fountains, and plenty of people to watch.
➕ F6 ✉ Nathan Road, Tsim Sha Tsui 🚇 Tsim Sha Tsui

THE HONG KONG RACING MUSEUM
This museum at the Happy Valley racecourse charts Hong Kong's love of horse-racing since the track was founded in 1884.
➕ G9 ✉ 2/F Happy Valley Stand Happy Valley Racecourse ☎ 2966 8065 🕓 Tue–Sun 10–5; Sun and public holidays 1–5. Race days 10–12:30. 🚊 Happy Valley tram from Central

POLICE MUSEUM
Exhibitions are concerned with the history of the Hong Kong police force, triads, and narcotics.
➕ F9 ✉ 27 Coombe Road, Wan Chai Gap ☎ 2849 7019 🕓 Wed–Sun 9–5; Tue 2–5 🚌 15 from Exchange Square

Just looking

There are plenty of places in Hong Kong where you can have some fun for free. It costs nothing to stand in a street market and watch the strange mix of modern bustle and ancient tradition that goes on all around you. Several small museums, including the Railway Museum in Tai Po, Flagstaff House in Hong Kong Park, and the Sheung Yiu Folk Museum in Saiking, are also free.

Kowloon Park

JOURNEYS

Stairway to heaven

Special to Hong Kong is the 15-minute trip up to the Mid Levels on escalators. The series of escalators begins in Central, on Des Voeux Road beside the central market, and extends through the heart of the city into suburbia. The covered escalators and walkways are on stilts above the streets, so you get a fascinating view of the life below.

Tram 8 to Kennedy Town

See Top 25 Sights for
PEAK TRAM (▶ 27)
STANLEY BY BUS NO. 6 OR 260 (▶ 48)
STAR FERRY (▶ 38)

FERRY TO CHEUNG CHAU
An air-conditioned first-class cabin with a bar and a sunny, open-air deck make this 40-minute ride past speeding catamarans, scruffy sampans, vast tankers, and tiny golden islands a relaxing treat.
➕ D7 ✉ Outlying Islands Ferry Pier, Central 🕐 Half-hourly 6:30AM–11:30PM 🚇 Central 🎫 Moderate

HELICOPTER RIDES
The ultimate in sightseeing—and it ought to be at these prices (HK$7,500 for five passengers on a 45-minute flight around Kowloon and the New Territories). Other trips can be arranged as well.
➕ E8 ✉ Heliservices, 2 Ice House Street, Central ☎ 2802 0200 🕐 By arrangement 🚇 Central 🎫 Expensive

SHEK O BY BUS NO. 9
Shau Kei Wan was once a tiny fishing village, but is now a suburb. The bus starts its journey from the Shau Kei Wan MTR station. The bus ride heads out east along Shek O Road, past Tai Tam Bay with the South China Sea beyond and green hills inland. You'll find some of the best beaches in Hong Kong in and around Shek O.
➕ M8 ✉ Bus terminus, Nam On Street, Shau Kei Wan 🕐 Every 15–30 minutes 🚇 Shau Kei Wan 🎫 Inexpensive

TRAM RIDE
For value, this has to be one of the best rides in the world. For HK$2.00 you can travel the length of Hong Kong Island from Kennedy Town in the west to Shau Kei Wan in the east on a double-decker tram. The top deck provides a bird's-eye view of the teeming life of Hong Kong Island.
➕ D7/M8 ✉ Central, Wan Chai
➕ Sheung Wan, Shau Kei Wan MTR
🕐 6AM–1AM 🎫 Inexpensive

COMPUTERS

COMPUTER MALL

A collection of specialist computer shops retailing hardware and software. Shops look more sophisticated than those in Sham Shui Po, but the selection is basically the same.

 G8  11–12/F, The In Square, Windsor House, 311 Gloucester Road, Causeway Bay  Daily 10–8  Causeway Bay

GOLDEN SHOPPING CENTRE

A few stores sell computer books in English. It used to be where locals went for pirated goods since the government crack down on the trade. Still, legitimate software programs are sold here for less than elsewhere.

 E2  Golden Shopping Centre, 146–52 Fuk Wa Street, Sham Shui Po  Daily 11–8  Sham Shui Po (follow signs for the Golden Shopping Centre)

LANG TEX

Good place if you are looking to repair or purchase new Apple computers or software. Unlike in other areas, you won't have a series of stores where you can comparison shop but you can call in advance to get answers before you make the trek to Wan Chai. It takes about to 20 to 30 minutes to walk to from Central Hong Kong; five minutes by taxi; 10 minutes by MTR, and 15 minutes by tram.

 F8  Room A, 3rd Floor, Thomas Commerical Centre, Thomson Road, Wan Chai  2728 0045  Call in advance  Wan Chai

MONG KOK COMPUTER CENTRE

This small shopping block is crammed with tiny shops that spill out into the teeming corridors. The vendors are knowledgeable and catalogs of prices are on display. Hardware is mostly Asian-made: computers, monitors, printers, and add-on boards. Warranties are usually only for Asia, but prices are competitive.

 F4  Mong Kok Computer Centre, 8–8a Nelson Street, Mong Kok  2781 1109  Daily 11–10  Mong Kok

NEW CAPITAL COMPUTER PLAZA

The concentration of computer stores is far less dense than at the nearby Golden Shopping Centre. Discounts of 10–20 percent on software can often be negotiated.

 E2  100–2 Yen Chow Street, Sham Shui Po  Daily 11–8  Sham Shui Po

THE NOTEBOOK SHOP

The entire second floor of Star House, known as Star Computer City, is devoted to computers and peripherals. This particular store stocks only laptop computers, including quality names such as Toshiba and IBM. Special offers are usually available.

 F6/F7  Unit A6–7, 2/F, Star House, 3 Salisbury Road, Tsim Sha Tsui  2736 7260  Mon–Fri 9:30–6:30; Sat 9:30–5:30  Tsim Sha Tsui

Shopping tips

Before parting with any money, check whether the warranty is an international one or just for Asia. If it is the latter, the price should be lower. Always check a quote with other retailers before making a substantial purchase. When buying software, make sure you know the specs of your hardward and check the minimum memory and speed requirements on the box before you buy. Prices in Hong Kong are comparable to those in the U.S.; Europeans will find some good bargains.

CAMERAS & ELECTRONICS

Shopping tips

Before you leave home, check prices on the kinds of items you may be tempted to buy. Despite Hong Kong's longstanding reputation as a source of low prices on camera and electronics, stickers can be higher than in the U.S. Avoid shops that do not display prices. Get quotes from various dealers and try haggling a little. Finally, if you do make a purchase, use a credit card, and watch carefully as your acquisition is put back into its box and then into a bag— many dealers won't take stuff back after you've left the store. Look for the HKTB logo displayed in stores; they also supply free special interest pamphlets including their *Official Shopping Guide* and shopping guides to buying electronics and jewelry.

BROADWAY PHOTO SUPPLY

This is the biggest branch of a Hong Kong-wide electronics and electrical chain that sells everything from washing machines to electric razors. Most major brands are available at marked down prices, which are more or less fixed, although you might get a free gift thrown in. You can get a good idea here of a sensible local price, and then move on to serious haggling in some smaller, pushier place if you really want to.

✚ F4 ✉ G/F and 1/F, 731 Nathan Road, Mong Kok ☎ 2394 3827 🕑 Mon–Sat 10:30–9:30; Sun 11:30–9:30 🚇 Mong Kok

FORTRESS

A major rival of Broadway offering a similar range of cameras, sound equipment, camcorders, electronics, electronic games, and so on, all at fixed prices. There are dozens of branches throughout the city, but this one is good for reconnaissance before setting off on a major haggling trip. Buy here and enjoy a hassle-free vacation, but if you like the cut and thrust of bargaining, then this should at least be your first stop.

✚ F6 ✉ Shop 281, Ocean Terminal, Harbour City, Canton Road, Tsim Sha Tsui ☎ 2735 8628 🕑 Mon–Fri 10:30–7:30, Sat, Sun and holidays 10–8 🚇 Tsim Sha Tsui

PHOTO SCIENTIFIC

Has a great reputation for good, if not cheap, prices for camera equipment and is especially liked by professional users. No bargaining here—pay up. This street has several other camera equipment shops, so if you want to shop around you don't have far to go.

✚ D8 ✉ G/F, 6 Stanley Street, Central ☎ 2522 1903 🕑 Mon–Sat 9–7 🚇 Central

WILLIAM'S PHOTO SUPPLY

A major competitor of Photo Scientific, this store also deals with cognoscenti. Again, you will find no great bargains, but if you are searching for that special something, it might just be here. Besides cameras there is the usual range of binoculars and the like.

✚ D8 ✉ 138B Prince's Building, 10 Chater Road, Central ☎ 2522 8437 🕑 Mon–Sat 10–6:30 🚇 Central

SHA TIN

This area out towards the racecourse is full of small electronics shops, as well as branches of the major electrical outlets. Prices are likely to be marked and fixed. You might also try the two department stores, Seiyu and Yaohan. Don't go on Sunday or you will find yourself among what seems like the entire population of the New Territories.

✚ Off map to north 🚇 Sha Tin

MEN'S CLOTHES

ASCOT CHANG

A Hong Kong shirt-making institution.

🕇 F6 ✉ Peninsula Hotel, Tsim Sha Tsui ☎ 2367 8319 🕓 Mon–Sat 9–7, Sun 9–5 🚇 Tsim Sha Tsui

CAUSEWAY BAY

This is a major shopping area, less touristy than Central or Tsim Sha Tsui. Here is the enormous Times Square mall (➤ 57) and four Japanese department stores—Matsuzakaya, Mitsukoshi, Daimaru, and Sogo—all with several designer outlets, Marks & Spencer is here, as are all the local chain stores and Lane Crawford, a classy Southeast Asian department store.

🕇 G8 🚇 Causeway Bay

THE LANDMARK

Men's stores here include Gentlemen Givenchy, Hugo, Ballantyne Boutique, Basile, Etienne Aigner, Jaeger, Benetton, Lanvin, Missoni, and the Swank Shop. Prices are worth comparing with those for the same names in the U.S. However, in the nearby Pedder Building, factory outlets sell the same labels at even lower prices (➤ 56, 77).

OCEAN CENTRE

This and the connecting malls have branches of Carpe Diem, Ermenegildo Zegna, Francescati, Gentlemen Givenchy, Hugo, Swank Shop, as well as an excellent Marks & Spencer and local chain stores such as Giordano, G2000, and U2.

🕇 F6 ✉ Harbour City, 5 Canton Road, Tsim Sha Tsui 🕓 Daily 10–8 🚇 Tsim Sha Tsui

PACIFIC PLACE

A collection of designer outlets and local chain stores. This mall has an Alfred Dunhill, Ermenegildo Zegna, Hugo, Swank Shop, plus a Marks & Spencer, Lane Crawford, and several local retailers selling casual separates at basic prices (➤ 56).

SAM'S

Another Hong Kong institution, numbering the Duke of Kent among its clientele.

🕇 F6 ✉ Burlington Arcade K, 92–4 Nathan Road, Tsim Sha Tsui ☎ 2367 9423 🕓 Mon–Sat 10:30–7:30, Sun 10–12 🚇 Tsim Sha Tsui

W. W. CHAN & SONS

Suits made by this very classy tailor have a lifespan of about 20 years and will be altered free of charge during that time. Once they have taken your measurements, you can order another suit from home.

🕇 F6 ✉ A2, 2/F, Burlington House, 94 Nathan Road, Tsim Sha Tsui ☎ 2366 9738 🕓 Mon–Sat 9–6 🚇 Tsim Sha Tsui

Made to measure

Perhaps the most distinctive aspect of men's clothes in Hong Kong is the number and quality of tailors and the excellent prices of their products compared to almost everywhere. If you intend to have a suit made in Hong Kong, you should make finding a tailor that you like a priority, since the more time and fittings he can have the better the suit will be: A good tailor can make a suit in as little as 24 hours, but a few days will yield a better, less expensive suit. Some tailors offer a mail order service. See Ascot Chang and W. W. Chan, left, and Irene Fashions (➤ 76).

If you have a suit that fits perfectly, you might want to ask the tailor to duplicate it.

WOMEN'S CLOTHES

Shop 'til you drop

The really swank place to go for women's clothes is the Landmark, where every big European name is represented, including Versace, Issey Miyake, Armani, Hermes, Loewe, and Nina Ricci. Other shopping centers (► 56–57) all have an interesting range of clothes and labels. Note that stores aimed more at the local market tend to stock smaller sizes and popular frillier styles with fur lining or sequins. Most local shoe stores don't stock sizes larger than 6 or 7.

CHINESE ARTS AND CRAFTS (HK) LTD., TSIM SHA TSUI

This shop sells the most glorious silk lingerie as well as embroidered *cheong sams* (a straight dress with a side slit), jackets, crocheted silk sweaters and shawls, and kimonos. Quality varies and cannot always be relied upon (► 70).

IRENE FASHIONS

This respected women's tailor takes several days and at least two fittings to make a suit. Have something you like copied, or choose the material and pattern at the shop.

➕ D8 ✉ Room 1102–3, 11/F Tung Chai Building, 86–90 Wellington Street, Central ☎ 2850 5635 🕐 Mon–Sat 9–6 🚇 Central

PACIFIC PLACE

Look for designer wear in Lane Crawford and Seibu department stores, T-shirts in local chain stores such as U2 and Giordano. Cotton Collection sells attractive cotton dresses, and Jessica has some elegant but inexpensive outfits (► 57).

STANLEY MARKET

Interesting stands sell all sorts of things, including discounted Monsoon clothes, sportswear, Indian prints, silk garments, funny T-shirts, and designer jeans.

➕ Off map to south ✉ Stanley 🚌 Bus 6 or 260 from Central Bus Terminal

TIMES SQUARE

When you have blazed through this mall, there is more shopping near by—in the streets around Causeway Bay, including Marks & Spencer, the electronics mega chain store, Fortress, and the Excelsior Hotel shopping arcade (► 57).

TOKYU

This reasonably priced department store has a whole arcade of local designer boutiques, as well as all the big names. Clothes range from young, inexpensive casuals to classy, costly evening gowns. There is also some good sportswear.

➕ F7 ✉ New World Shopping Centre, Salisbury Road, Tsim Sha Tsui ☎ 2722 0102 🕐 Daily 10–9 🚇 Tsim Sha Tsui

VINCENT SUM DESIGNS

A handicraft shop that stocks lots of interesting and pretty batik cloth as well as clothes made from ethnic prints.

➕ D8 ✉ 15 Lyndhurst Terrace, Central ☎ 2542 2610 🕐 Daily 10–6 🚇 Central

VOGUE ALLEY

A whole shopping center dedicated to boutiques of local-designers. Predominantly young clothes.

➕ G8 ✉ Paterson and Kingston Streets, Causeway Bay 🚇 Causeway Bay

FACTORY OUTLETS

AH CHOW FACTORY

Chinese pottery and tableware, often very good quality or seconds. Nearby are clothing factory outlets such as Mia Fashions at 680 Castle Peak Road, well worth a look.

✚ C1 ✉ Block B, 7F, 1 and 2 Hong Kong Industrial Centre, Castle Peak Road, Lai Chi Kok ☎ 2745 1511 ⏰ Daily 10–6 Phone for appointment 🚇 Lai Chi Kok

DIANE FREIS FACTORY OUTLET

This well-known local designer's factory sells dresses and evening gowns at about 30 percent off.

✚ H5 ✉ 41 Man Yue Street, Hung Hom ☎ 2362 1760 ⏰ Mon–Sat 9:30–6:30. Closed Sun 🚇 Tsim Sha Tsui then taxi

FA YUEN STREET

Better known for its street market (▶ 54), this is also home to a series of factory outlet shops. Labels are usually cut out, but you can find Marks & Spencer, Laura Ashley, Next, Saks, Victoria's Secret, and many other European and U.S. clothes at reductions of around 50 percent (or more).

✚ F3 ✉ Fa Yuen Street, Mong Kok ⏰ Daily 10–6 🚇 Prince Edward

HUNG HOM

The Kaiser estates are two blocks of mainly clothing factories, many with stores inside. The factories make clothes for department stores all over the world and their stores sell seconds or overruns with the labels cut out. There are also jewelry outlets here. However, this is not a leisurely place to shop. Be prepared to dig through piles of clothes and trek through the blocks of Hung Hom. Wear sensible shoes.

✚ G5–H5 🚇 Tsim Sha Tsui then taxi

LAN KWAI FONG

Several boutiques and shops sell clothes at reduced prices in this area, notably CCC, Gat, and Whispers; all stock some well-known names at good prices.

✚ D8 ✉ Central 🚇 Central

PEDDER BUILDING

Five floors of tiny shops, all with something worth poking around in. Not all are factory outlets, and some sell both regular designer stuff and discounted items, so browse carefully.

✚ D8 ✉ 12 Pedder Street, Central 🚇 Central

TIMOTHY FASHION

Both men's and women's clothes. Good buys vary from season to season—look for woolen sweaters in fall, silk shirts and dresses in summer.

✚ H5 ✉ Kaiser Estate, Phase 1, 41 Man Yue Street, Hung Hom ☎ 2362 2389 ⏰ Mon–Sat 9:30–6:30 🚇 Tsim Sha Tsui then taxi

Bargain bazaars

There are two major areas to look for bargains—in the Pedder Building on Hong Kong Island for the real big names, and around the factories themselves in Hung Hom in Kowloon. Granville Road in Tsim Sha Tsui is another place full of small shops selling anything from junk to amazing bargains, but you have to be dedicated to find the really good things. What you are likely to find is samples, seconds, and overruns, often with the labels cut out. Women's clothes come mainly in small sizes, but sometimes larger bodies are catered for.

SPORTS

Away from it all

If you stay in Hong Kong long enough—and this may be just days, or even hours— the need to escape the crowds and enjoy some recreation becomes irresistible. Take a jog along Bowen Road (➤ 16) at any time of the day, an early morning or late evening jog along the Waterfront Promenade in Tsim Sha Tsui (➤ 18), or a run up Victoria Peak (➤ 27). The Hash House Harriers (☎ 2376 2299) also organize regular runs.

SWIMMING

There are sandy beaches with safe swimming that are netted-off (to ward off shark attacks—although sometimes beaches close for shark alerts), but the beaches are very crowded on weekends, and hence, often polluted. Lifeguards are on duty from April to September.

CHEUNG SHA
✉ Lantau Island ⛴ Outlying Islands Pier, Central, then bus from Silvermine Bay

DEEP WATER BAY
✉ South side of Hong Kong Island 🚌 7 from Central Bus Terminal to Aberdeen, then 73

REPULSE BAY
✉ South side of Hong Kong Island 🚌 6, 61 from Central

SHEK O
✉ Southeast side of Hong Kong Island 🚌 9 from Shau Kei Wan

SILVERSTRAND
✉ Sai Kung Peninsula, New Territories 🚇 Choi Hung then bus 92 or taxi

STANLEY BEACH
✉ South side of Hong Kong Island 🚌 6, 260 from Central Bus Terminal

GOLF

CLEARWATER BAY GOLF AND COUNTRY CLUB
A par-70, 18-hole, pro championship course. The golf course has stunning views.
✉ Lot #227 in DD 241, Po Toi O, Sai Kung, New Territories ☎ 2719 1595 🕑 Mon–Fri 7:30–6 🚇 Choi Hung MTR, then bus 92 ✋ Green fees HK$1,400

DISCOVERY BAY GOLF CLUB
You need a whole day to enjoy a game at this 18-hole layout on outlying Lantau Island (➤ 14, 24).
✉ Valley Road, Discovery Bay, Lantau Island ☎ 2987 7273 🕑 Mon–Fri 8:30–3.15 ⛴ Outlying Islands Pier, Central ✋ Green fees HK$900

HONG KONG GOLF CLUB
The famous golf club with a 36-hole course has practice putting greens. Three additional (more expensive) 18-hole courses are at Fanling, New Territories (☎ 2670 1211), and are also open to visitors.
✉ 19 Island Road, Deep Water Bay, Hong Kong Island ☎ 2812 7070 🕑 May–Aug Mon–Fri 9:30–2:30. Sep–Apr Mon–Fri 9:30–1:30. Closed first Tue of every month 🚌 minibus 6 from Central Bus Terminal ✋ Green fees HK$600

JOCKEY CLUB KAU SAI CHAU PUBLIC GOLF COURSE
There are two, 18-hole courses designed by Gary Player and a driving range at this public golf course.
✉ Kau Sai Chu, Sai Kung, New Territories ☎ 2791 3380 🕑 Daily 7AM–8PM 🚇 Choi Hung MTR, then bus 92or Green Minibus No. 1A to Sai Kung Bus Terminal. Proceed to the waterfront where you board the golf course's ferry for Kai Sai Cha ✋ Green fees HK$350–900

NIGHTCLUBS

CATWALK

This glitzy entertainment complex with disco and karaoke rooms stars 11 bands from around the world and has a resident Latin American salsa band, and a video wall. Free midweek; cover charge Thu–Sat.

✚ F7 ✉ New World Hotel, 22 Salisbury Road, Tsim Sha Tsui ☎ 2369 4111 ext 6380 🕐 Sun–Thu 9:30PM–3AM; Fri–Sat 9:30PM–4AM 🚇 Tsim Sha Tsui

CLUB ING

Draws chic young Hong Kong girls, this place tries to bill itself as *très* chic, but many say it's missing the mark. Still it's packed every weekend.

✚ F8 ✉ 4/F, New World Harbour View Hotel, 1 Harbour Road, Wan Chai ☎ 2824 1066 🕐 Daily 9:30PM–3AM 🚇 Wan Chai

INSOMNIA

Crowds sometimes make dancing a chore. Check out the expat crowd at the bar—they often spill out onto the street.

✚ D8 ✉ Ho Lee Commercial Building, 34–36 D'Aguilar Street, Central ☎ 2525 0957 🕐 Mon–Sat 8AM–2AM; Sun 2PM–5AM 🚇 Central

JJs

This club has a pizza lounge, pool table and dart board, and a house band that consistently plays to enthusiastic audiences. Happy hours 5:30PM–8:30PM. Dim sum 6PM–7:30PM.

✚ F8 ✉ Grand Hyatt Hotel, 1 Harbour Road, Wan Chai ☎ 2588 1234 🕐 Mon–Thu 9:45PM–2AM; Fri–Sat 10PM–3AM; Sun 9PM–2AM 🚇 Wan Chai

JOE BANANAS

Very trendy American-style bar, disco, and restaurant. Long hours on weekends; men must wear a shirt with collar. Happy hours 11AM–9PM.

✚ F8 ✉ 23 Luard Road, Wan Chai ☎ 2529 1811 🕐 Daily Mon–Thu 11AM–5AM; Fri–Sat 11AM–6AM; Sun and holidays noon–4AM 🚇 Wan Chai

MINE

A cavernous club that draws crowds for hard-hitting house music.

✚ F8 ✉ 2441 Lockhart Road, Wan Chai ☎ 2267 8822 🕐 Mon–Thu 5PM–4AM; Fri 5PM–6AM; Sun 8PM–6AM 🚇 Wan Chai

NEPTUNE

Live music and DJs entertain multiracial dancers. The cover charge varies with the season and the day, but in general this place offers the most dancing for the least money.

✚ F8 ✉ 98–108 Jaffe Road, Wan Chai ☎ 2865 2238 🕐 Daily 9PM–7AM 🚇 Wan Chai

POST '97

Sultry Moroccan-style café, bar, and club, open 24 hours on weekends.

✚ D8 ✉ UG/F Cosmos Building, 9–11 Lan Kwai Fong, Central ☎ 2810 9333 🕐 Mon–Thu 9AM–2AM; Sat 9AM–Sun 9AM 🚇 Central

Cover charges

Always telephone discos before you go to confirm the hours and cover charge. Many places have reduced rates during the week and/or include one or two drinks in the price. Expect to pay HK$100+ on Friday and Saturday.

LIVE MUSIC

Nightlife on the island

Lan Kwai Fong, in Central, is where the see-and-be-seen crowd spends their money on over-priced drinks. Wan Chai, once seedy, is now one of the hippest nightlife areas in town. Soho (south of Hollywood Road) is a popular dining and drinking area for expats. Stanley is unique—more relaxed and meditative than other areas.

CARNEGIE'S

An interesting nightspot where the music shifts genre regularly but is often from local bands. The music is loud and there's usually a crush on the dance floor. Cover charge only for men on weekends.

F8 ✉ 53 Lockhart Road, Wan Chai ☎ 2866 6289
🕐 Thu 7PM–10PM; Sat 7PM–midnight; Sun 7PM–11PM
Wan Chai

DELANEY'S

The design recreates a Victorian Irish general store-cum-pub, and there's live traditional music and Irish food—even Guinness. In the branch in Luard Road, there is a Sunday evening jam session.

F6 ✉ G/F, Multifield Plaza, 3–7a Prat Avenue, Tsim Sha Tsui ☎ 2301 3980
🕐 Mon–Thu noon–3AM; Fri–Sat noon–5AM; Sun noon–2AM
Tsim Sha Tsui
Also at
F8 ✉ 2/F, 18 Luard Road, Wan Chai ☎ 2804 2880
🕐 Mon–Thu noon–3AM; Fri–Sat noon–5AM; Sun noon–2AM
Wan Chai

HARDY'S FOLK CLUB

Not as folksy as its name suggests but still a viable alternative to the heavy metal, rock, and jazz venues. Come just for a drink, or have a meal.

D8 ✉ 35 D'Aguilar Street, Central ☎ 2522 4448
🕐 Daily 5:30PM–2AM
Central

THE JAZZ CLUB

Too many places in Hong Kong are squashed into anonymous buildings, but the cramped confines here are just what is required. The Jazz Club, one of the few places you can count on for quality jazz, regularly features musicians from all over the world; drinks are reasonably priced, and cover charges, high for big names, are dropped for local acts. Seats can be reserved but must be claimed before 9PM on weekends. The alternative atmosphere and lively audience make for a great night out.

D8 ✉ 2/F, California Building, 34–6 D'Aguilar Street, Central ☎ 2845 8477
🕐 Daily 9:30PM–2AM
Central

NED KELLY'S LAST STAND

The best place in Hong Kong for traditional and Dixieland jazz, belted out by a resident band. Expect a convivial atmosphere, pub food, and no cover charge.

F6 ✉ 11a Ashley Road, Tsim Sha Tsui ☎ 2376 0562
🕐 Daily 9PM–2AM
Tsim Sha Tsui

THE WANCH

Sociable and deservedly popular place, this former folk club, now has rock instead—usually very good music indeed. Reasonably priced as well, so things can get crowded, arrive early. No cover charge.

F8 ✉ 54 Jaffe Road, Wan Chai ☎ 2861 1621
🕐 Daily 9PM–2AM
Wan Chai

BARS/PUBS

ACROPOLIS
There's no music at this dedicated watering hole, but a sociable set of customers often fills the place to capacity.
✚ D8 ✉ G/F, Corner 11 Tower, 21 D'Aguilar Street, Central ☎ 2877 3668 🕐 Daily 11AM–3AM 🚇 Central

BREZEL HAUS
A pub that looks and feels very German. When you step inside, if you want, you can check your English at the door and dive into a hearty conversation about Munich and Berlin.
✚ D8 ✉ 23 Hollywood Road ☎ 2451 5449 🕐 noon–11PM 🚇 Central

BULL & BEAR
This British-style setting, with oak beams and English bar food, is very popular with expatriate office workers during happy hour (5–8 weeknights). No live music.
✚ E8 ✉ G/F, Hutchinson House, 10 Harcourt Road, Central ☎ 2525 7436 🕐 Mon–Sat 8AM–2AM; Sun noon–midnight 🚇 Admiralty

DICKENS BAR
A Dickensian place that's one of Hong Kong's best and most deservedly fashionable bars. Bands change constantly—Irish, West, Indian, Indonesian, and Filipino—and there's trumpet-blasting jazz Sunday afternoons.
✚ G8 ✉ LG/F, Excelsior Hotel, 281 Gloucester Road, Causeway Bay ☎ 2894 8888 🕐 Mon–Sat noon–1:30AM; Sun 3PM–midnight 🚇 Causeway Bay

THE DUBLIN JACK
Packed with regulars on weekends, this friendly place fills to overflowing towards the end of the week, as it's *the* established pub for Central office workers. You'll always find good *craic* (conversation).
✚ D8 ✉ 37–43 Cochrane Street (next to escalator), Central ☎ 2543 0081 🕐 Daily 11AM–12.30AM 🚇 Central

MAD DOGS, KOWLOON
This cosmopolitan bar attracts tourists and locals alike. Live music Tuesday, Thursday, Sunday; happy-hour 4–8 every evening.
✚ F6 ✉ 32 Nathan Road, Tsim Sha Tsui ☎ 2301 2222 🕐 Mon–Thu, Sun 8AM–2AM; Fri–Sat 8AM–4AM 🚇 Tsim Sha Tsui

OSCAR'S
Very trendy, fan-cooled bar opening on to the street. The food is good in the separate restaurant, but the main activity is amiable drinking and chatting.
✚ D8 ✉ G/F and basement, 2 Lan Kwai Fong, Central ☎ 2804 6561 🕐 Mon–Sat 11AM–2PM; Sun 11AM–midnight 🚇 Central

STAUNTON'S WINE BAR & CAFÉ
Packed to the gills most nights, this bar by the Soho escalators remains one of the most popular in town. The glass doors make it perfect for people-watching.
✚ D8 ✉ 16A Staunton Street ☎ 2869 7652 🕐 Daily 11AM–11PM 🚇 Central

Nightlife in Kowloon
Because of its budget accommodations, Kowloon has lots of inexpensive, casual bars, many with an Australian flavor, such as the Kangaroo, overlooking Kowloon Park, and Ned Kelly's. In addition, there are the many hostess bars, where a drink and a girl to talk to come in a package. Some of these, including Bottoms Up in Hankow Road, are almost a national institution.

LUXURY HOTELS

Prices

For a double room per night expect to pay:

Luxury
over HK$1,000

Mid-Range
HK$700–HK$1,000

Budget
under HK$700

HONG KONG ISLAND

CHARTERHOUSE

A pleasant little hotel tucked away in Wan Chai. Lots of facilities, near major shopping areas. Compact but very comfortable rooms.

G8 ✉ 209–19 Wan Chai Road, Wan Chai ☎ 2833 5566; fax 2833 5888; e-mail www.charterhouse.com Ⓜ Causeway Bay or Wan Chai

CONRAD INTERNATIONAL

Rooms are spacious and individually designed with every comfort. Some of the best views in Hong Kong are from the amazing top floors. Fitness center, pool, and beautiful interiors.

E8 ✉ Pacific Place, 88 Queensway ☎ 2521 3838; fax 2521 3888; e-mail www. conrad. com.hk Ⓜ Admiralty

THE EXCELSIOR

Pleasant and casual with nice rooms and an enormous range of facilities, right down to the two covered tennis courts on the roof. Convenient to shopping and nightlife.

G8 ✉ 281 Gloucester Road, Causeway Bay ☎ 2894 8888; fax 2895 6459; e-mail mandarin-oriental.com/ Ⓜ Causeway Bay

J.W. MARRIOTT

A pleasant and peaceful place to stay in the heart of Central, near major tourist attractions and with plenty of facilities. Spacious, sunny rooms, all with two floor-to-ceiling glass walls. Outdoor pool, fitness center.

E8 ✉ Pacific Place, 88 Queensway ☎ 2810 8366; fax 2845 0737; e-mail www.conrad.com.hk Ⓜ Admiralty

MANDARIN ORIENTAL

The very central Mandarin Oriental has a long tradition of impeccable service. Well-appointed rooms, with superb attention to detail. Helpful staff, classy shopping center, great pool, excellent restaurants.

E8 ✉ 5 Connaught Road, Central ☎ 2522 0111; fax 2810 6190; e-mail mandarin--oriental.com/ Ⓜ Central

RENAISSANCE HARBOUR VIEW

A very modern, bright hotel with glass walls and a prime location; the high floors have harbor views. Spacious rooms, pleasantly appointed. Enormous fitness center and swimming pool. There is even a rooftop jogging track.

F8 ✉ 1 Harbour Road, Wan Chai ☎ 2802 8888; fax 2802 8833 Ⓜ Wan Chai

KOWLOON

THE PENINSULA

A landmark, cultural icon, and tourist attraction in its own right, this is the last word in style. Very popular afternoon tea.

F6 ✉ Salisbury Road, Tsim Sha Tsui ☎ 2366 6251; fax 2722 4170; e-mail www.peninsula.com/phk.htm Ⓜ Tsim Sha Tsui

MID-RANGE HOTELS

HONG KONG ISLAND

FURAMA

This Central hotel is perfect for business travelers and shoppers. For best views, ask for a room above the 17th floor. Expect fine dining in all of the restaurants. Top end of mid-range.

➕ E8 ✉ 1 Connaught Road ☎ 2525 5111; fax 2845 9339 🚇 Central

GRAND PLAZA

Connected to the Tai Koo MTR station, it has a vast recreational facility and plenty of shopping nearby. However, it is not as centrally located as other options.

➕ K8 ✉ 2 Kornhill Road ☎ 2886 0011; fax 2886 1738 🚇 Tai Koo

NEW HARBOUR

Only minutes from the MTR station and bus and tram routes to the east and west.

➕ F8 ✉ 41–9 Hennessy Road, Wan Chai ☎ 2861 1166; fax 2865 6111 🚇 Wan Chai

THE WESLEY

Close to train, tram, and bus routes, with a café and decent international restaurant.

➕ F8 ✉ 22 Hennessy Road, Wan Chai ☎ 2866 6688; fax 2866 6633 🚇 Wan Chai

KOWLOON

EATON

Large with a range of room rates, as well as restaurants and a bar (but no pool or sports amenities). Catch any bus stopping outside the door to get to Tsim Sha Tsui.

➕ F5 ✉ 380 Nathan Road, Yau Ma Tei ☎ 2782 1818; fax 2782 5563 🚇 Jordan

IMPERIAL

There are no restaurants or nightlife here, but you don't need them when you are at this end of Nathan Road.

➕ F6 ✉ 30–4 Nathan Road, Tsim Sha Tsui ☎ 2366 2201; fax 2311 2360 e-mail reservation@imperialhotel.com.hk 🚇 Tsim Sha Tsui

INTERNATIONAL

In the heart of Tsim Sha Tsui, with reasonable restaurants and rooms with balconies and neon views.

➕ F6 ✉ 33 Cameron Road, Tsim Sha Tsui ☎ 2366 3381; fax 2369 5381 🚇 Tsim Sha Tsui

THE SALISBURY

This 366-room YMCA has a lot going for it: a location that's convenient to shopping and the Star Ferry, plus an inexpensive self-service restaurant and free use of a swimming pool.

➕ F6 ✉ 41 Salisbury Road, Tsim Sha Tsui ☎ 2369 2211; fax 2739 9315 🚇 Tsim Sha Tsui

SHAMROCK

A good-value no-frills hotel with an economical restaurant. Buses are on the doorstep, and you're close to the MTR.

➕ F5 ✉ 223 Nathan Road, Yau Ma Tei ☎ 2735 2271; fax 2736 354; e-mail shamrock@iohk.com 🚇 Jordan

Hotel tips

A travel agent should be able to obtain sizable discounts on the room rates in the luxury and mid-range hotels and may offer special winter rates to attract customers. Try to get a breakfast buffet included because it is often a substantial repast.

85

BUDGET ACCOMMODATIONS

Chungking Mansions

Chungking Mansions, a vast, crumbling and dingy shopping and housing high-rise on Nathan Road, used to be raided regularly by the police in search of illegal immigrants and, as a result, has such an image problem that the budget accommodations there have never quite been able to recover despite the fact fire regulations are now enforced and unlicensed premises have been closed down. Although the elevators remain claustrophobic and the stairways are even worse, it is still the best place in town to look for budget rooms—and budget Indian restaurants (➤ 66).

HONG KONG ISLAND

GARDEN VIEW INTERNATIONAL HOUSE (YWCA)

The only budget hotel-style accommodation on Hong Kong Island with an outdoor swimming pool (closed in winter). Reserve in advance.

✚ D9 ✉ 1 MacDonnell Road, Central ☎ 2877 3737; fax 2845 6263 🚌 12A from Central Bus Terminal or minibus from outside City Hall

NEW CATHAY

Expensive end of the range with few facilities but a good location. Single rooms are the best value because, unusually among Hong Kong hotels, they cost considerably less than doubles.

✚ H8 ✉ 17 Tung Lo Wan Road, Causeway Bay ☎ 2577 8211; fax 2576 9365 🚇 Causeway Bay

NOBLE HOSTEL

A reliable establishment offering rooms with both shared and private bath. A double with private bathroom at HK$340–$HK360 is a gem of a bargain on Hong Kong Island.

✚ G8 ✉ Flat A3, 17/F, 27 Paterson Street, Causeway Bay ☎ 2576 6148; fax 2577 0847 🚇 Causeway Bay

KOWLOON

BOOTH LODGE

Named after the founder of the Salvation Army, (which operates the place). This hotel is well-run, with clean rooms, efficient service, and a small café.

✚ F5 ✉ 11 Wing Sing Lane, Yau Ma Tei ☎ 2771 9266; fax 2385 1140 🚇 Yau Ma Tei

CARITAS BLANCHI LODGE

Tidy, clean, well-run, and friendly. Facilities are limited, just a laundry and restaurants.

✚ F5 ✉ 4 Cliff Road, Yau Ma Tei ☎ 2388 1111; fax 2770 6669 🚇 Yau Ma Tei

CARITAS LODGE (BOUNDARY STREET)

Basic and roomy with a coffee shop, laundry facilities, and some triple rooms.

✚ G3 ✉ 134 Boundary Street, Kowlooni ☎ 2339 3777; fax 2338 2864 🚇 Prince Edward, then bus 2D

KING'S HOTEL

Reasonably priced and pleasant rooms well suited for a walk into Tsim Sha Tsui. Close to MTR. The restaurant serves Western, Chinese, and Thai food. You'll also find a coffee shop and laundry service.

✚ F4 ✉ 473–473A Nathan Road, Yau Ma Tei ☎ 2780 1281; fax 2782 1833 🚇 Yau Ma Tei

YMCA INTERNATIONAL HOUSE

This modern block has 300 rooms with basic amenities at competitive rates. No membership required.

✚ F4 ✉ 23 Waterloo Road, Yau Ma Tei ☎ 2771 9111; fax 2388 5926 🚇 Yau Ma Tei

HONG KONG
travel facts

ARRIVING & DEPARTING

Before you go

- All U.S. citizens, even infants, need a valid passport to enter Hong Kong or Macau for stays of up to three months.
- No vaccinations are required.

When to go

- The ideal time is between October and mid-December— days are warm and fresh, nights cool and comfortable.
- If you have a choice, avoid June–September, when the weather is uncomfortable with high humidity.

Climate

- Spring and fall are usually warm, but spring is more unsettled, with rain common.
- Winters are usually comfortable, although there are occasional cold spells when a jacket or light coat is essential.
- Summer is very hot and humid, with nearly 16inches (400mm) of rain on average each month. The clammy heat sometimes gives way to violent typhoons.

Typhoons

- Called hurricanes in the Atlantic, typhoons (from *dai foo*, the Chinese for "big wind") hit Hong Kong between July and September. There is a well-rehearsed procedure for dealing with these storms, and hotels post the appropriate storm signal:
- Storm Signal 1: Typhoon within 500 miles of Hong Kong.
- Storm Signal 3: Typhoon on its way, be prepared.
- Storm Signal 8: Stay in your hotel; dangerous winds with gusts.

Arriving

- All flights land at Hong Kong's international airport, Chek Lap Kok,which is 23 minutes by rail from Central, 18 minutes from Kowloon.
- Take the shuttle to the Airport Express railroad station or to the taxi rank.
- There are public buses, hotel buses, and a hotel shuttle bus service, as well as taxis and the train, but the train is the most efficient and pleasant way of getting to town.

Customs regulations

- The duty-free allowance is 1 liter of spirits and 200 cigarettes.
- Export and import licenses are required for any amount of ivory taken out of the country.

Departure tax

- Anyone over 12 years old pays HK$100. Payment in Hong Kong dollars only. This is usually included in the price of our airline ticket. Check with your travel agent.

ESSENTIAL FACTS

Electricity

- The current is 200/220 volts, 50 cycles alternating current (AC).
- Most wall outlets take three square prongs; some older ones take three large round prongs.
- U.S. appliances require a converter and a plug adapter.

Etiquette

- Hong Kong is a fast city, so don't be surprised when people push, shove, and jump the lines or fail to line up at all.
- Shaking hands with either sex is common practice and the

exchanging of business cards, presented with both hands, is even more common.

- Chinese names begin with the family name, so Mr. Tan Wing Chan, for example: is Mr. Tan; the adoption of a Western first name is very common.
- A service charge is usually added to restaurant bills, but the waiting staff do not get this money as tips, so an extra 10 percent is expected. Always round up taxi fares to the next dollar or two.

Lone travelers
- For lone travelers Hong Kong is similar to, and often safer than, European or North American cities; take commonsense precautions.
- Public transportation at night is as safe as during the day.

Money matters
- Travelers' checks can often be used as payment or cashed at banks or moneychangers. Always check the exchange rate before making any transaction; banks offer the best rates.
- Credit cards—Visa, Access (MasterCard), American Express, and Diners Club—are widely accepted for purchases in stores and restaurants. In small shops make sure commission is not being added—this is illegal.
- Credit cards can be used to obtain cash from banks and ATM machines. Some Hong Kong Bank teller machines provide 24-hour HK$ withdrawal facilities for Visa and MasterCard holders. Amex holders have the same facility at some Jetco ATMs, as well as the Express ATMs.

National holidays
Dates of the Chinese lunar festivals vary from year to year.
- Jan 1: New Year's Day.
- Late January or early February: Chinese New Year.
- Good Friday and Easter Monday.
- Early April: Ching Ming Festival.
- Mid-to-late June: Dragon Boat Festival.
- Early or mid-August: Sino-Japanese War Victory Day.
- Late September or early October: Mid-Fall Festival.
- Mid-to-late October: Cheung Yeung Festival.
- December 25 and 26: Christmas Day and Boxing Day .

Opening hours
- Offices: Mon–Fri 9–5; Sat 9–1.
- Banks: Mon–Fri 9–4:30; Sat 9–12:30.
- Post offices: Mon–Fri 8–6; Sat 8–2.
- Stores: Daily 10–6, often 10–9 in tourist areas.

Places of worship
- Protestant Evangelical Community Church ✉ 4th floor YMCA, Salisbury Road, Tsim Sha Tsui ☎ 2369 2211
- The Roman Catholic Cathedral ✉ 16 Cairn Road, Mid Levels, Hong Kong Island ☎ 2810 4066
- Jewish Ohel Leah Synagogue ✉ 70 Robinson Road, Central ☎ 2857 6095
- Kowloon Mosque ✉ Kowloon Park ☎ 2724 0095

Restrooms
- Most restrooms are Western style.
- Hotels are the best places to find clean restrooms.
- In older places and on transportation, the MTR and

KCR, restrooms are often of the squat type common in Asia.
- Always carry a packet of tissues. You can purchase (these are sold at newsstands for HK$1 or HK$2).

Student travelers
- There are few discounts for ISIC (International Student Identity Card) holders.
- For a free booklet detailing retail outlets with student discounts, see the Student Travel Bureau ✉ Room 1021, 10/F, Star House, Tsim Sha Tsui ☎ 2730 3269
- Some places of interest have a reduced student admission.

Time differences
- During daylight savings time Hong Kong is 13 hours ahead of the New York City, 16 hours hours ahead of Los Angeles and San Francisco.

Tourist information
- The Hong Kong Tourist Board (HKTB) has two offices:
  ✉ Star Ferry Concourse, Tsim Sha Tsui
  🕐 Mon–Fri 8–6; Sat, Sun, public holidays 9–5
  ✉ Shop 8, Basement, Jardine House, Connaught Place, Central 🕐 Mon–Fri 9–6; Sat 9–1
- For telephone information:
  ☎ 2807 6177 Mon–Fri 8–6; Sat, Sun, public holidays 9–5

PUBLIC TRANSPORTATION

Buses
- Traveling by bus is not recommended (except for trips to the south side of Hong Kong Island); the MTR (Mass Transit Railway) is faster and easier.
- The fixed fare is marked on the bus as you enter and pay; no change is given.

- Red and yellow minibuses carrying 14 to 16 passengers can be flagged down almost anywhere along their routes.
- Green and yellow maxicabs also carry 14 to 16 passengers, but stop only at designated places.
- For a short stay, it is not worthwhile to master the system of minibuses and maxicabs.

Taxis
- The flagfare is HK$15 and after about a mile (2km) the fare increases by HK$1.40 for every 210 yards (200m). There is a HK$5 additional charge if a taxi is reserved by phone and comes to your pick-up point.
- Using one of the tunnels between Hong Kong Island and Kowloon costs from HK$20 to HK$45, depending on which tunnel is used.
- A "For Hire" sign is displayed in the windscreen; at night a "Taxi" sign is lit up on the roof.
- Taxis technically are not supposed to stop at bus stops or on a yellow line.
- Taxis are good value, but most drivers don't speak much English. Most taxis have a card with the top 50 destinations listed in Cantonese, English, and Japanese. However, it's worth having your destination written down in Chinese.

Trains
- The MTR is the quickest way to hop between shopping areas, between Hong Kong Island and Tsim Sha Tsui; for access to the New Territories use the interchange station at Kowloon Tong and change to the KCR (Kowloon–Canton Railway), which travels north to the

border at Lo Wu.
- Stations are located by a symbol and there are clear instructions in English for operating machines.
- Machines issue thin plastic tickets, available at machines or at information/ticket counters.
- Fares are between HK$4 and HK$12.50.
Information ☎ 2881 8888

Trams
- Trams run only on Hong Kong Island's north side—but the route between Kennedy Town in the west and Causeway Bay in the east is useful.
- Destinations are marked on the front in English.
- The fixed fare of HK$2 is dropped in the paybox when leaving the tram.

Travel discounts
- For the MTR, KCR, buses, some ferries, and several other forms of public transportation, you can buy an Octopus ticket which you can buy and recharge as often as you want at any ticket office—and save yourself having to search around for change for bus journeys and line up for tickets in the busy MTR. For HK$150, you get a little over HK$100 worth of travel. (the other HK$50 is refundable when you leave). Check your ticket balance at any railroad station or look at the machine as you go through the barrier. Further discounts are available for students, senior citizens, and children.

Where to get maps
- MTR maps are available at the airport and most hotel lobbies.

- MTR stations dispense a free guide.
- HKTB offices (➤ 90) have a free map showing bus routes and fares.

MEDIA & COMMUNICATIONS

International newsdealers
- International newspapers and magazines are available in bookstores, hotel kiosks, and newsstands on street corners.
- The sidewalk newsdealer outside the Star Ferry terminal in Tsim Sha Tsui and the bookstore next to the ferry terminal in Central have a good selection.

Magazines
- *Time*, *Newsweek*, *The Economist*, and the regional *Asiaweek* are widely available.
- The *Far East Economic Review* is best for business and news.
- For entertainment listings look for the free, bi-weekly *HK Magazine* or *BC Magazine*.

Newspapers
- There are two English-language daily newspapers: *South China Morning Post* and *Hong Kong iMail*. The *SCMP* is a broadsheet while *iMail* is a tabloid format.
- International papers with Asian editions are the *Asian Wall Street Journal*, *USA Today*, and the *International Herald Tribune*.

Post offices
- The General Post Office on Hong Kong Island is next to the Star Ferry Concourse in Central.
- In Kowloon, the main post

office is at 10 Middle Road, off the lower end of Nathan Road.

- Letters and postcards to destinations outside Southeast Asia cost HK$3.10 for the first 10g, plus HK$1.20 for each additional gram.
- The Speedpost service cuts the usual five-day service to Europe or North America by about half.

Radio

- Daily English-language newspapers give details of station wavelengths and programs.

Television

- There are two English-language stations—Television Broadcast (TVB) Pearl and Asia Television Limited (ATV) World and two Cantonese-language stations.
- Many hotels subscribe to Rupert Murdoch's Star TV satellite television.

Telephones

- Public phones charge HK$1 per call and sometimes they only take HK$2 coins and do not give change. By pressing the "FC" (follow-on call) button before hanging up you can make a second call.
- Phonecards, available in denominations of HK$50, HK$100, and HK$250 at 7–Eleven stores and in many shops, are easier to use, especially for International Direct Dial calls.
- Some phone booths accept only phonecards or only coins; others accept both.
- For IDD calls, dial 001, followed by the country code and then the area code (minus

any initial 0) and the number. Dial 013 for information about international calls.

EMERGENCIES

Emergency phone numbers

- Police/Fire/Ambulance ☎ 999

Embassies and consulates

- Australia ✉ 23rd and 24th Floors, Harbour Centre, 25 Harbour Road, Wan Chai ☎ 2827 8881
- Canada ✉ 11th–14th Floors, Tower One, Exchange Square, 8 Connaught Place, Central ☎ 2810 4321
- Germany ✉ 21st Floor, United Centre, 95 Queensway, Central ☎ 2105 8788
- U.K. ✉ c/o Overseas Visa Section, Immigration Department, 2nd Floor, Wan Chai Tower Two, 7 Gloucester Road, Wan Chai ☎ 2824 6111
- U.S.A. ✉ 26 Garden Road, Central ☎ 2523 9011

Lost and found

- ✉ Admiralty MTR station ⏰ Mon–Sat 8–7 ☎ 2861 0020

Medical treatment

- Casualty departments of public or private hospitals provide emergency treatment.
- Private doctors (see "Physicians and Surgeons" in the Yellow Pages) charge HK$150 per visit on average. This usually includes three days' medication.
- Public hospitals: Queen Mary Hospital ✉ Pok Fu Lam Road, Hong Kong Island ☎ 2855 3111 Queen Elizabeth Hospital ✉ Wylie Road, Yau Ma Tei, Kowloon ☎ 2958 8888 Kwong Wah Hospital ✉ 25 Waterloo Road, Yau Ma Tei, Kowloon ☎ 2332 2311
- Private hospitals: Hong Kong Central ✉ 1B Lower Albert Road, Central, Hong Kong Island ☎ 2522 3141 Adventist ✉ 40 Stubbs Road, Wan Chai,

Hong Kong Island ☎ 2574 6211
Baptist ✉ 222 Waterloo Road,
Kowloon Tong ☎ 2337 4141

Medicines

- Watson's and Manning's are the biggest chain stores dispensing medicines (see "Chemists" in the Yellow Pages) and are usually open until 8PM.
- A full range of pharmaceuticals is readily available.

Sensible precautions

- Hong Kong is very crowded, night and day, and professional pickpockets and thieves capitalize on this.
- Keep wallets and purses secure.
- Keep travelers' checks separate from the invoice that lists their numbers.
- Don't leave valuables where you can't see them at all times.
- Keep travel documents and money in a hotel safe.

LANGUAGE

- Hong Kong has two official languages: English and Cantonese. English is spoken widely in business circles and in tourist areas, but not every Chinese person understands English as many have come to live here from mainland China. To avoid any confusion and frustration, get the hotel receptionist to write down your destination in Chinese.
- You may come across some unfamiliar English words in Hong Kong: *amah*, housekeeper or servant; *chop*, a personal seal used in business; *dai pai dong*, street food stand; *godown*, warehouse; *wet market*, a fresh food market; *congee*, a porridge made from rice.

- A few words of Cantonese go a long way in establishing rapport—and off the beaten track they may prove useful.

Can you speak English? neih wuih mwuih gong ying mahn?
good morning jóu sahn
how are you? néih hou ma?
hello (only on the phone) wai! (pronounced "why")
thank you (for a favour) mgòi
thank you (for a gift) dò jeh
please mgòi
excuse me mgòi
I'm sorry deui mjyuh
yes haih *or* hou
no mhaih *or* mhou
where? bin douh?
how many/how much? géi dõ?
how much is it? géi dõ chin?
airport fèi gèi chèung
bus bã si
tram dihn chè
what time is it? géi dim jung?
three o'clock sáam dim jung
tea chàh
sugar tòhng
beer bè jáu
dollar mãn
U.S. dollar méih gàm
Peak Tram Laahm Chè
The Peak Sàn Déng

0	leng	20	yih sahp
1	yãt	21	yih sahp yat
2	yih	30	sàam sahp
3	sàam	31	sàam sahp yat
4	sei	40	sei sahp
5	ngh	50	ngh sah
6	luhk	60	luhk sahp
7	chát	70	chát sahp
8	baat	80	baat sahp
9	gáu	90	gáu sahp
10	sahp	100	yãt baak
11	sahp yãt	1,000	yãt chihn

93

INDEX

Citypack
Hong Kong

AUTHORS *Sean Sheehan and Pat Levy*
UPDATED BY *Lara Wozniak*
CARTOGRAPHY *Automobile Assication Developments Limited/RV Reise- und Verkehrsverlag*
COVER DESIGN *Fabrizio La Rocca, Tigist Getachew*
COVER PHOTOGRAPHS *Hong Kong Tourist Association*
MANAGING EDITOR *Hilary Weston* INDEXER *Marie Lorimer*

Copyright   © Automobile Association Developments Limited 1996, 1999, 2001
Maps copyright   © Automobile Association Developments Limited 1996, 1999, 2001
Fold-out map   © RV Reise- und Verkehrsverlag Munich · Stuttgart
                   © Cartography: GeoData

Published in the United Kingdom by AA Publishing

ISBN 0–679–00692–3
Third Edition

Acknowledgments

The Automobile Association wishes to thank the following photographers, libraries, and associations for their assistance in the preparation of this book:
Art Directors amd Trip Photo Library 58; Museum of History, Hong Kong 39a, 39b. Rex Features Ltd 12. Spectrum Colour Library 5b, 21a, 49b, 87b. Museum & Art Gallery, University of Hong Kong 26. Travel Ink/Derek Allan 24; World Pictures 24a, 24b. The remaining pictures are held in the Association's own library (AA Photo Library) and were taken by Alex Kouprianoff with the exception of pages 13a and 20, which were taken by Ingrid Morejohn.

Important tip

Time inevitably brings changes, so always confirm prices, travel facts, and other perishable information when it matters. Although Fodor's cannot accept responsibility for errors, you can use this guide in the confidence that we have taken every care to ensure its accuracy.

Special sales

Fodor's Travel Publications are available at special discounts for bulk purchases (100 copies or more) for sales promotions or premiums. Special editions, including personalized covers, excerpts of existing guides, and corporate imprints, can be created in large quantities for special needs. For more information, contact your local bookseller or write to Special Marketing, Fodor's Travel Publications, 280 Park Avenue, New York, NY 10017. Inquiries from Canada should be directed to your local Canadian bookseller or sent to Random House of Canada, Ltd., Marketing Department, 2775 Matheson Blvd. East, Mississauga, Ontario L4W 4P7.

Origination by BTB Colour Reproduction Ltd, Whitchurch, Hampshire
Manufactured by Dai Nippon Printing Co. (Hong Kong) Ltd
10 9 8 7 6 5 4 3 2 1

Titles in the Citypack series

- Amsterdam - Beijing - Barcelona - Berlin - Boston - Brussels & Bruges -
- Chicago - Dublin - Florence - Hong Kong - Lisbon - London - Los Angeles -
- Madrid - Melbourne - Montreal - Munich - New York - Paris - Prague -
- Rome - San Francisco - Seattle - Shanghai - Singapore - Sydney - Tokyo -
- Toronto - Venice - Vienna - Washington D.C. -